TO THE
Faithless
AND THE UNBELIEVING
BERTRAM GREY

TO THE
Faithless
AND THE UNBELIEVING
BERTRAM GREY

KEVIN GARRETT

Copyright © 2025 by Kevin Garrett

All rights reserved. No part of this publication may be reproduced, distributed, or transmitted in any form or by any means, including photocopying, recording, or other electronic or mechanical methods, without the prior written permission of the copyright owner and the publisher, except in the case of brief quotations embodied in critical reviews and certain other noncommercial uses permitted by copyright law. For permission requests,write to the publisher, addressed "Attention: Permissions Coordinator," at the address below.

ARPess
45 Dan Road Suite 5
Canton, MA 02021

Hotline: 1(888) 821-0229
Fax: 1(508) 545-7580

Ordering Information:

Quantity sales. Special discounts are available on quantity purchases by corporations, associations, and others. For details, contact the publisher at the address above.

Printed in the United States of America.

ISBN-13:	Softcover	979-8-89676-337-6
	eBook	979-8-89676-338-3
	Hardback	979-8-89676-339-0

Library of Congress Control Number: 2024927238

CHAPTER 1

Jacob Lent was a good Christian man.
He loved his God and he loved his Church. He loved his family, he loved his friends, and he did his best to love his enemies. He read his Bible daily and strove to keep The Commandments, as Jesus had said, in his heart. He happily tithed ten percent of his pay and faithfully attended Church Services three times a week, once on Tuesday, twice on Sunday, and sometimes more often, as the seasons required.

He had a sticker on the back bumper of his car that read:

> Jesus is Lord,
> The Bible said it,
> I believe it,
> End of Discussion!

He would quote it whenever he felt someone might be trying to test his faith or sow within him some seed of doubt, but he was blessed in that way, for doubt was never an ailment from which he suffered. Even as a child, Jacob had always been certain of his place in Creation—who he was, why he was, what he would do with his life. It was more than simple faith, more than simply saying that he believed. He *knew* what he believed was true.

And Jacob Lent knew many things.

He knew how the universe was created and that it took only six days to make. (Whether that happened six thousands years ago or six billion years ago did not matter). He knew that Adam and Eve were the first two people on Earth, and that every person alive today was a descendant of that bloodline. He knew that there was a Heaven and that there was a Hell, and that Heaven was all happiness and bliss, and that Hell was all fire and brimstone.

He knew that every decision ever made came down to only two choices, either good or evil. He knew that all things of God were good and that all things of Satan were evil. He knew that each person was born with an immortal soul, which was endowed with the ability to choose its own fate, and that the Ultimate Fate of all souls was either Eternal Salvation or Eternal Damnation. Salvation was good. Damnation was evil. But the most important thing that Jacob Lent knew was that Jesus Christ was the only Path to Salvation.

Of course with such all-encompassing knowledge came a great moral responsibility—namely to share it with as many people as would listen, and in their listening perhaps find Salvation. But Jacob discovered, more often than not, that those people most in need of saving were often times the ones most vigorously opposed to being saved, and many times he found himself being accused of arrogance and condescension.

He found this perplexing.

After all, did one whisper a warning at a blind man who was about to step out in front of a speeding car? No, of course not! The warning must be shouted, and shouted with authority, if it was to be heard and taken seriously. Yet, he found that most people did not care to be spoken to in so urgent a manner, even when such urgency was appropriate, but since it was the fate of other men's souls that was at stake, Jacob Lent learned to whisper his warnings instead of shouting them. Surprisingly, he found that this worked much better. A Persistent Humility, as he came to call it, for Blessed are The Meek as the Beatitudes said, and it was true for he saved many a lost and wayward soul in this quiet and diligent manner.

But even as good as he was, Jacob Lent knew that most souls were doomed to eternal suffering. Jesus spoke of it often in his teachings and Jacob testified to it no less frequently—for many are invited, but few are chosen, and the lost will be thrown into The Lake of Fire, where there will be weeping and gnashing of teeth.

Only the righteous could enter the Kingdom of Heaven. Jacob could only set the example, show the way. The soul had to be free to make its own choice. Jacob knew this. And yet whenever a soul did make the wrong choice despite his best efforts, Jacob could not help but feel personally responsible for the loss, for he knew that it was never God's intention to see anyone suffer the eternal torments of Hell. Therefore, the fault must be his own.

It was this overwhelming sense of responsibility to God and to his Fellow Man that eventually caused Jacob to leave his job as junior assistant manager of The Good Word (the smaller of the three Christian Book Stores in the modest town of Pietyville, South Carolina) and to enter into a full time position under the services of God as Pastor of The Temple Creek Baptist Church and Christian Youth Academy. He was a very happy man, happy in his world, happy in his life, happy in the good fortune that God had given him. But life wasn't always about happiness.

God had a Plan.

To the Faithless and the Unbelieving BERTRAM GREY

And quite often, good and faithful men had to suffer through various tests so that this Plan could be realized. Jacob Lent was himself, just this sort of man—faithful, honest, worthy of being tested—and God would test him.

But life was a complicated process, and sometimes the work of faithful men alone was not enough to ensure that God would succeed in His Designs, and so He had to rely on the actions of the faithless and the unbelieving to get the job done. And there was no one more faithless and unbelieving than Jacob's nephew—an inquisitive and introspective boy of twelve, who doubted every thing that could not be proven and trusted no one but himself. His name was Bertram Grey.

Bertram Grey was a quiet thoughtful child, an earnest and diligent student who sought to learn all the lessons that the world had to teach him, both in and out of his elementary school classroom. One of the most important things that the world had taught Bertram was about people.

People, Bertram had learned; even those with good and kind intentions weren't always the most dependable creatures on Earth. They had problems, all kinds of problems, and he found that it was usually best to try to rely on himself to get what little he needed in life, rather than to surrender his fate to the whims of unpredictable people with problematic lives.

Bertram's mother (who had problems too) taught Bertram this valuable lesson while he was still in kindergarten. He was very glad to have learned it at such an early age because it prepared him for the day, years later, when she left him, quite suddenly and without much warning, on the front porch of Jacob's house. She left him there alone, with two paper sacks full of clean clothes, a smaller plastic grocery bag containing a peanut butter sandwich and a banana, a toothbrush and a comb, and a note in a sealed envelope.

The note said this:

"Dearest Brother: This is my son Bertram. Please look after him while I am away. He is a quiet boy and very well behaved. You should have no problem with him. I know this is sudden and I am very sorry I did not call first, but something has come up that I need to fix and it's best if I do it alone. Don't worry. Everything is going to be fine. I'll get in touch with you as soon as I am settled again. Talk to you soon. Hope all is well."

The note was signed: "Love You Bunches. Your Favorite Sister, Gertrude."

Bertram's mother had not allowed Bertram to read this note before sealing it into the envelope and placing it into the plastic grocery bag, but Bertram liked neither mysteries nor surprises, and he could tell by her mood that something unpleasant was about to happen. So he retrieved the envelope while she wasn't looking, opened it, and read the note for himself. Then he placed the note into a new envelope identical to the first, and returned it to the plastic grocery bag before she had a chance to notice that it was missing.

Bertram never told his mother what he had done because he kept thinking that she would eventually explain everything to him before leaving him with his uncle, but that never happened. Instead, she simply kissed his cheek, told him that she loved him, and said that she would return for him soon.

She also told him that it was very important for him to wait ten minutes after she had gone before knocking on the front door of the house, because although her brother was a kind and generous man, he was also very stubborn, and she knew that he would insist on her staying the night before traveling on. But time permitted no delays for reasons she did not fully explain. Reasons, she said, her brother would never understand. Bertram did not understand either, but he did as he was told.

He waited.

And as he waited, he began to notice how quiet it was, standing there alone on the front porch of his uncle's house, and how late in the day it was becoming. He began to worry that whoever might be inside the house might be busy eating supper or relaxing on the sofa after a hard day at work, and he started to think how unfair it would be to inconvenience them by making them get up to answer the door. So he waited thirty minutes more than his mother had told him in order to give whoever might be inside enough time to finish what they were doing and to, hopefully, come out of the house on their own accord. Maybe they would need to take out the trash, he hoped, or to put the cat out for the night (if they had a cat), and then he wouldn't have to disturb them by knocking.

But no one came to the door.

And now, after waiting much longer than his mother had told him, it was even later in the day. The sun had set. The moon was slowly creeping out over the treetops and the sky was growing darker by the minute. Bertram tried peering through a window to see if he could see anyone inside, but the curtains were drawn and the lights were out and he couldn't see a thing, which caused him to worry that whoever might be inside might have already gone to bed for the night. And rather than cause a commotion at so late an hour, Bertram began to think that it might be best just to wait until morning before attempting to knock on the front door.

After all, he was safe and in no real danger. The air was cool but still pleasant. If it did get any colder later in the night, he had two paper sacks full of clothes that he could use to keep warm. He could put on an extra shirt and pants and he could wear white cotton tube socks on his hands as mittens. There was even a perfect place on the porch for him to sleep, a large wooden porch swing that hung to the left of the front door from the ceiling on white painted chains. He went to the swing and sat on it to test its strength, rocked gently back and forth on it as he looked upward and watched the movement of the chains. All seemed well. Now all he needed was a comfortable pillow on which to rest his head and he could settle in for the night and go to sleep.

Fortunately, this was not a problem either.

He knew exactly what to do. He hopped off the swing, rummaged through his paper sacks, and selecting various articles of clothing from each sack, he set them in a pile at one end of the swing. When he was satisfied that he had enough materials to work with, he began trying various combinations of socks, pajama bottoms, underwear, and T-shirts to see which would make the most practical and comfortable kind of pillow.

He eventually settled on a pillow made by rolling two pairs of pants together to form a tube—the inside layer denim blue jeans, the outside layer cotton sweat pants. He mashed it flat to adjust its height and tested its comfort by putting it on his shoulder and resting his cheek against it. It felt good against his face and he was satisfied that it would work, so he set it aside and carefully folded all of the other clothes that he had tried but did not use and put them back into the sacks. He rolled the tops of the sacks closed, slid them beneath the porch swing and picked up the pillow again.

He was standing in front of the swing, studying it to determine which end would be most suited for placing the pillow when suddenly the front porch light came on and the screen door opened.

A man stepped out from behind the door and onto the porch.

"Hello," Bertram said to the man.

"Hello," the man said. "I thought I heard someone out here. May I help you?"

Bertram had never seen his uncle before, and his mother had not told him what his uncle looked liked, but the man on the porch did seem by all outward appearances to be a kind and generous person, which gave Bertram some optimism that the man might be his uncle. That is, if Bertram's mother hadn't mistakenly dropped Bertram off at the wrong house, which was quite possible, though he hoped that was not the case. But hope was not a thing that Bertram relied upon. Hope was too much like having faith or wishing on a star.

And Bertram trusted neither stars nor faith.

Bertram found that knowing was always better than hoping, no matter how harsh or difficult the truth. The man standing before him now was either his uncle or he was not. Hoping about it made no difference. Facts were facts. Hope did not change them. And the only way to know the facts, in this case, was to ask the man his name. But the man, seeing the paper sacks beneath the swing and the improvised pillow still in Bertram's hand, interrupted Bertram with a question of his own, before Bertram had a chance to gather the courage to know the truth and to face the facts as they were.

The man said, "Planning on camping out tonight?" His tone was familiar in some way, reassuring and firm, yet humble at the same time.

"No," Bertram said to the man. "I wasn't planning to."

"It's a good night for it," the man said, "but isn't it a little late to be out when there's school tomorrow? Does your mother know where you are?"

"Yes," Bertram said. "She does."

"Then she must have sent you here? Do you need to borrow something? A loaf of bread? Some eggs? Or maybe a cup of sugar?"

Bertram did not know what to say, so he said nothing.

The man said, "You don't have to be embarrassed to ask for something if you need it. We all need things from time to time. God put us together on this Earth to help one another out."

Bertram had often heard people saying this same thing about God and people helping people, though he had never been entirely convinced that it was true. But the man did seem honest and sincere about the way he said it, and Bertram felt that even if the man was not his uncle, the man might still be able to help him in some way, and so Bertram ventured to ask his question. "Is your name Jacob Lent, and do you have a sister named Gertrude Lent?" Bertram said.

"Yes," the man said quietly. He seemed surprised. "My name is Jacob Lent and I do have a sister named Gertrude. Why do you ask?"

"Because I am your nephew. My name is Bertram Grey."

"Oh yes," Jacob said as if remembering something that he had forgotten. "We've been expecting you."

And now it was Bertram's turn to be surprised. "You have?" he said. Bertram knew that his mother had not called, because he had read the note in the envelope, but his uncle was insistent. He was so insistent, in fact, that Bertram began to wonder if he had misread the note. "Are you sure?" he said.

Jacob laughed. "I hope it was her. Otherwise there's somebody else calling me on the phone who sounds just like her and claims to have a son named Bertram who's going to be staying with us for a while. You don't have a twin brother, do you?"

"No sir."

"Then I guess you must be the Bertram Grey she was talking about."

"I guess so," Bertram said. He was still a little confused about what was happening, and so he did what he always did when he was confused; he asked a question. "Do you remember what she said exactly?" Bertram said.

"Well no, not exactly. I don't think I ever remember anything exactly. In fact, your showing up here tonight kind of proves that. I thought she said she'd be dropping you off next week, not this week."

"When she called you?"

"Yes."

"And when was that?" Bertram said.

"Oh, I'm afraid I don't remember that exactly either, sorry. Sometime last week I think. Or maybe it was last month, towards the end. I've been very busy lately. I must have gotten the dates mixed up. I guess I should have written it down. I hope I haven't kept you waiting too long out here on the front porch."

And then Bertram understood what was happening. He recognized the vagueness of a hastily told lie. There had been no mix up, and he had not been invited. It was just as the note in the envelope had said; his mother had not called, and his uncle had not been expecting him next week, this week, or any other week for that matter. The truth was that his uncle was lying to him, but Bertram understood that it was a lie told out of kindness to make him feel welcomed and to spare his mother's reputation, and so Bertram returned the kindness with a lie of his own, just to be polite.

Bertram said, "No, I haven't been waiting long at all. I just got here."

"Good, then let's get you inside. I'll bet you're probably a little tired and would like to get some sleep." Jacob stooped down to gather up the paper sacks beneath the swing, but Bertram stopped him.

"Wait," Bertram said. "There's a letter. My mother said to give it to you when you answered the door so you could read it."

"I'm sure it can wait. I'll read it later."

"She said it was important to give it to you when you answered the door."

"Oh? Okay then," Jacob said and he stepped aside as Bertram knelt beside the swing and pulled out one of the paper sacks to open it.

"It's in here," Bertram said and he took the envelope from the plastic grocery bag and gave it to Jacob. Jacob took the envelope, folded it in half with one hand, and slid it into the right back pocket of the denim blue jeans he was wearing. He was about to stoop down again to pick up the remaining sacks, when Bertram stopped him again.

"Aren't you going to read it?" he said.

"Once we're inside. I'm sure it can wait."

"Maybe you should read it now," Bertram suggested.

"I will, as soon as we're inside. The light's better in there and I'll bet you're probably a little hungry too? I think there's some leftover pie in the refrigerator. You could have a piece before you go to bed tonight. Would you like that?"

"No thank you," Bertram said. "I'm not really hungry, but maybe you should read the letter before you go inside. She said it was important."

"Very well," Jacob said, sensing Bertram's uneasiness. "I'll read it now if you like." Jacob withdrew the envelope from his pocket and opened it up. He was keenly aware, as he did so, that every gesture he made and every expression that flashed across his face was being carefully scrutinized by his young nephew. And so, as Jacob read the letter silently to himself, he was careful to keep his outward appearance as casual and undisturbed as it would have been had he been reading a birthday card or the entertainment section of the evening newspaper.

He had scarcely finished with the letter and had not even looked up from his sister's signature at the bottom of the page, when he heard Bertram's voice in a slightly strained and nervous pitch. "Is everything okay?" Bertram said.

"Yes, fine. Now let's get you inside."

"Did you read it all?"

"Yes."

"Then it wasn't too important?"

"No, not at all."

"What did it say?"

"Nothing much, you know, the usual stuff that people say in letters—hello, goodbye, how's it going—that kind of stuff. We'd just finished talking on the phone a week or so before, so I guess she didn't have much to say."

"Then it's okay for me to stay—I mean—then it wasn't too important?"

"No, not too important at all," Jacob said again, and then he knelt in front of Bertram so that he could look directly into his eyes and he said, "Like I told your mother over the phone, 'We are happy to have you in our home and you are welcomed to stay with us for as long as you wish.'"

"Thank you," Bertram said simply, "for inviting me."

"You're welcome," Jacob said. "Now, are you sure you're not just a little bit hungry for some pie?"

"Maybe just a little bit."

"Good. I thought you might be. Now let's get you inside."

Jacob made one final attempt to pick up the paper sacks beneath the swing, but Bertram had them in his arms before Jacob had a chance to reach for them.

"Would you like any help with that?"

"No thank you," Bertram said. "I've got them."

"Very well," Jacob said, and he pulled the screen door open and he held it in place so that Bertram could go inside.

THE NOT UNWELCOME GUEST

Soon.

It was a word that Bertram never really liked.

Maybe because its meaning was too vague. Or maybe because it didn't seem to mean what he thought it was supposed to mean.

"When is Father coming home?" Bertram would ask his mother when it was quiet and they were alone.

"Soon," she would tell him.

But Father never came.

"When are they going to turn the lights on again?" Bertram would ask her when it was dark and the electricity didn't work.

"Soon," she would say. On one such occasion Bertram remembered how the word "soon" lasted almost three days, and that was quite a long time for the television and the hot water heater not to be working.

"When will we find a place to stay so we don't have to keep moving all the time and leaving our friends?" Bertram would ask her whenever he got tired of packing his things into paper sacks and cardboard boxes so they could find another place to live.

"Soon. I just have to find the right job and the right place."

But "soon" never happened.

"Don't worry. Everything is going to be fine," the letter in the envelope had said. "I'll be in touch with you as soon as I am settled again. Talk to you soon."

"Soon."

It was that word again.

So Bertram wasn't very surprised when this particular "soon" never happened either. He wasn't even disappointed about it because he knew that his mother had never been very good at keeping the big promises that she made to him, even when she did her best to try to keep them. In fact, the night she left him on Jacob's front porch, Bertram had been fairly certain that he would never see her again.

And he had been right.

He never did.

But he still thought fondly of her and hoped one day that she would call because he knew that she had not purposely abandoned him. She had simply lost her way and had forgotten how to get back to him, that was all. She loved him, he knew that, and he knew that if there had been a way for her to reach him, then she would have found it. But that was how she was, gentle and loving, and easily confused by maps and written directions that explained how to get to places where she had never been.

By contrast, Bertram saw how his Uncle Jacob never seemed lost or confused as he traveled from one place to the next, even without a map. Bertram wondered how his uncle and his mother could be so different when they were both brother and sister. But then Bertram remembered how identical twins could be very different too, and so he decided that maybe it was not so surprising after all.

Jacob's wife, however, she very much was a surprise for Bertram. Her name was Elizabeth Lent. She looked nothing like Bertram's own mother, but her mannerisms were strikingly similar, the serious nature in which she kept house, the way she told her not-so-funny-jokes, the sound of her voice in the morning when she first woke up, even the way she smelled.

Bertram found later that she used the same soap and the same perfume as his own mother, which amazed him even further. And sometimes, but not too often, if he closed his eyes, Bertram could almost pretend that she was his mother.

Bertram was very fond of his aunt, but he was careful not to call her Mom or Mother out of respect for the memory of his own mother. He simply called her Aunt Elizabeth, or sometimes Auntie Liz. Sometimes, but not too often. As for his Uncle Jacob, Bertram kept to calling him just that, Uncle or Uncle Jacob, but not out of respect for his own father, because Bertram never knew his father.

Bertram had a cousin named Billy, but Billy was three years older than Bertram and had his own circle of friends, so Bertram didn't call Billy much of anything. Mostly, Bertram just tried to stay out of Billy's way.

There was also a family cat named Mr. Boots that Bertram saw flashes of from time to time, outside in the yard, up a tree, beneath the porch chasing mice. Bertram never managed to get close enough to the cat to even touch it, much less to pick it up and to pet it, so he gave up trying. It wasn't a very friendly cat.

But despite Mr. Boots, this was Bertram's new family.

It was a good family, Bertram thought. He liked being part of it, even if he did not feel like he was a part of it, no matter how often his Uncle Jacob told him that he was. They were all Lents: Jacob Lent, Elizabeth Lent, and Billy Lent. Even his mother was a Lent, Gertrude Lent, but he was not. He was a Grey. Bertram Grey. Named after his father, his mother had told him once a long time ago.

Although Bertram knew that he was a relative by blood and that he really was part of their family in some remote way, he still felt more like a guest in the house—an unexpected though certainly not unwelcome guest, but a guest just the same. And as a guest, Bertram felt obligated to earn his keep as best he could, though it was difficult because he wasn't old enough to get a job. So he helped by doing odd jobs around the house and contributed financially by doing whatever he could to save his relatives money on the extra things that they were forced to buy for him to keep him clothed and fed.

Saving on food was simple enough. Bertram never took second helpings at the dinner table, and because he believed dessert to be a frivolous and unnecessary menu item, he accepted it only under special circumstances such as birthdays, or holidays, or sometimes when he felt that refusing it might offend his Aunt Elizabeth's generosity. When he did accept it, however, he was always careful to take the smallest piece on the platter so as not to deprive his Cousin Billy, who was very fond of dessert, the enjoyment of a late evening snack while watching one of his favorite TV shows.

Bertram was still growing, so saving money on what they spent to keep him clothed was a little more difficult, but he did what he could. He avoided schoolyard fights and rough games that might cause his pants to become stained or prematurely worn. If they did go shopping to buy him new clothes Bertram always chose the next larger size. When his aunt pointed out that they were much too big for him, Bertram told her that everyone was wearing them that way. It was the style, he said.

She seemed to believe him.

Bertram's feet, however, were a more serious problem. Bertram kept a very close watch on them. He measured them weekly and made a conscious effort to keep them exactly the same size as the shoes he wore. This way his uncle and his aunt would never have to buy him new shoes before he had a chance to completely wear out the old ones. But feet, Bertram discovered, grew pretty much as they pleased despite his best efforts. Even so, he still kept trying.

Luckily, Billy was taller than Bertram, and had much larger feet as well, which meant that Bertram usually got to wear his cousin's hand-me-downs. And that was good, for it meant that Bertram's uncle rarely ever had to spend money to buy Bertram new clothes or new shoes, which saved Bertram much guilt over the years.

But food and clothes were not the only things that had value.

"Time is money," he had often heard people say. He had heard it said on the radio and on the television, and even once or twice he had heard his uncle say it, which meant that it must be true. So to ensure that his presence did not cost his Aunt Elizabeth any time from her usual duties, Bertram made sure to always keep his room neat and his things put away. This was not the only reason that he was so meticulous about keeping his room clean. There was another more important reason.

Bertram understood that his room was not really his room. Not in the way that his Cousin Billy's room was his room. Bertram's room was the guestroom. It was a place Bertram was being allowed the privilege to stay until he was old enough to make his own way in the world, and he was very thankful for that, for he knew that there were many people in the world who had a lot less.

Bertram was mindful of the needs of his Cousin Billy as well. Bertram knew that children required love and discipline from their parents. Children needed to know that their parents cared about what they said and did, and not wanting to deprive his Cousin Billy of any of the attention due to him by his own parents, Bertram made sure that he did nothing to interfere with that relationship. Bertram always got his chores done on time and he always finished his homework before going outside to play.

After all, Bertram's Uncle Jacob and his Aunt Elizabeth were just that, his uncle and his aunt, not his parents. It would have been unfair to force them to divide their attention between himself and his Cousin Billy, especially when his Cousin Billy was clearly a problematic child and in far more need of the added attention than he was. Bertram was glad to see him get it too.

But as well intentioned as all of Bertram's plans were, he soon found that it caused a problem that he had not previously considered. Bertram had become so well mannered and so mature a child that his Uncle Jacob and his Aunt Elizabeth began using him as the standard by which to judge the conduct of all the children of the world. Unfortunately this category also included his Cousin Billy.

"Why can't you be more like Bertram?" he heard his Aunt Elizabeth say to his cousin one day. "Bertram makes his bed everyday," she said. "Bertram always gets good grades. Bertram never gets into fights. He is such a good little boy." Bertram was very happy to hear that his Aunt Elizabeth approved of his behavior, but the vicious stares and the quiet taunts he received from his cousin when no one else was around made Bertram realize that things could suddenly become very bad if he continued down his altruistic path of noble intentions. He knew something must be done.

And soon.

Happily, the solution was a simple one. Bertram began with small things first, like leaving toys and books and shoes lying out in the middle of the guestroom floor. Instead of putting his dirty clothes in the wash hamper as he used to, Bertram began piling them in a heap behind the guestroom door, just as his cousin did in his own room. Twice a week Bertram would leave his bed unmade so that his Aunt Elizabeth would have to make it for him, and when he did make it, he was always careful to leave enough lumps and wrinkles in it so that she would have to do a respectable amount of adjusting and smoothing before it would be presentable to any guests of social importance.

Sometimes Bertram would pretend to neglect his chores just to give his Aunt Elizabeth the opportunity to remind him, but more importantly, to give his Cousin Billy the opportunity to hear him being reminded.

As part of his new strategy in domestic harmony, Bertram would choose to break things from time to time, not because he wanted to, but because his Cousin Billy would often break things too. His Cousin Billy broke the living room lamp while play wrestling with a friend. His Cousin Billy broke the window on Mr. Sweeney's car while throwing rocks at the street lamp on the corner. His Cousin Billy broke his father's favorite pocket watch while trying to see how tight he could wind it without breaking it. This was not to say that his Cousin Billy was a malicious child, only a little reckless and accident prone as most children his age were.

Bertram, however, rarely ever broke anything by accident, because he was neither reckless nor careless; he could not afford to be. So when Bertram did break the things that he broke, he would have to break them on purpose. He broke nothing expensive or important, of course; a chipped plate, a mismatched drinking glass, something that could be easily fixed or that was of little value, like one of his Cousin Billy's old toys.

The only problem with this solution was that the punishments he would receive as a result of these planned delinquencies, were as equally inconsequential as the things he broke. His Aunt Elizabeth might say to him, "Be a little more careful next time," or, "Watch what you're doing. You might have cut yourself."

And that would be it, his punishment.

Nothing more than a gentle scolding.

It was very disappointing.

One year his Cousin Billy was put on restriction for an entire month—one week for skipping his Math class to avoid taking a final exam, another week for lying about it, and later, two more weeks for getting caught smoking a cigarette in the boy's bathroom.

Bertram soon realized that it would be impossible for him to surpass such a record without eventually compromising his own sense of right and wrong, but he did what he could and he hoped that his occasional, though minor, planned truancies might help to demonstrate to his uncle and to his aunt that he was no better a child than Billy, and that Billy was no worse.

In school, though capable of above average work, Bertram kept his grades at a level just below what Billy would earn in order to defuse another potential source of conflict between himself and his cousin. Grades were, after all, only a measure of how much a person understood what he was being taught. Bertram knew that he understood the things he was learning in school and he knew that he could have gotten higher marks on his papers if he had wanted them, and for Bertram, that was enough.

Families were more important than straight "A" report cards and first place ribbons in spelling, and Bertram did not want to humiliate his cousin by making him feel dull or stupid in the eyes of his parents. Jealousy between children for the favor of their parents was a terrible thing and Bertram did not want to be responsible for turning his cousin into a bully by forcing him to compete in a contest that he could never win. It would have been immoral for Bertram to cause trouble for people who had only shown him generosity and kindness, and that meant his Cousin Billy, as well.

THE PROBLEM WITH THE SOLUTION

Elizabeth Lent was the first to notice Bertram's new approach to domestic harmony because she was the one who had to remake his bed and pick up his toys and put his dirty clothes in the wash hamper. When she told Jacob about it and suggested that he counsel the boy to find out what might be troubling him, Jacob only laughed gently and kissed her on the forehead. "Good," he said. "I'm glad to see that he's finally beginning to feel at home."

"Good? Why can't children be happy and well adjusted and neat all at the same time?" she said. "When I was a child I was well adjusted and I always made my bed and I always put my things where they belonged."

"That's not the way it usually works."

"I know," she lamented, "but talk to him anyway. If something is troubling him, we need to find out what it is and try to help him. He's such a thoughtful little boy. I worry about him sometimes."

"I will talk to him," Jacob said and he kissed her forehead once again.

"Thank you," she said. "Now, what would you like for dinner tonight?"

THE FIRST QUESTION

Jacob talked to Bertram later that day and found that Elizabeth had been wrong. Bertram was not troubled. He was just thinking.

"Thinking? About what?" Jacob said.

"I have a question."

"Ask it. Maybe I can help you find the answer."

"I was hoping you could," Bertram said, "but I wasn't sure if I should ask."

"You can ask me anything you want, anytime you want," Jacob said.

Bertram stopped to think about this too, because his mother had also told him this, and Bertram knew from experience that it was best not to ask her some questions about some things, and that sometimes it was best not to ask her anything at all. But his uncle seemed genuinely concerned about his question and so Bertram decided to ask it. "Tell me, Uncle," Bertram said, "why is it that some people can believe in God and some people cannot believe?"

"That is a good question," Jacob said.

"That's why I wanted to ask you about it," Bertram said. "You are a preacher. You know about the Bible and you know about God. I was thinking you might know the answer."

"Yes, as a matter of fact I do know the answer."

Bertram was very happy to hear this. "Then tell me," Bertram said. "I want to know it too."

"The answer is simply this," Jacob said. "Everyone can believe in God if that is what they choose to do because God has given every person a measure of faith. What each person decides to do with that faith is up to him. It is our choice to believe or not to believe."

"Are you sure?"

"Yes."

"Oh," Bertram said, his initial excitement somewhat deflated. "I see. So some people choose to believe in God and others choose not to believe?"

"Yes."

"But if they choose not to believe, then they will go to Hell?"

"Yes. That is true."

"But why would anyone choose to go to Hell?"

"Why do some people choose to do good and others choose to do evil?" Jacob said. "It's because the Devil tempts us and if we follow these temptations, we stray from God, and when we stray from God, we sin."

"But why do some people stray and others do not?"

"Because some people are weaker than others."

"Why doesn't God make all of us strong enough not to stray? Unless God wants some of us to fail?"

"No, He doesn't want that, Bertram."

"Then why do they fail? Why must some people go to Heaven and others go to Hell?"

"They go to Hell because they make the wrong choices."

"Because they stray from God?"

"Yes."

"Oh," Bertram said again.

"Is something wrong?"

"No, it's just that it doesn't seem to explain anything. People stray from God because they're weak, but God made them like that, and so they go to Hell, but then God doesn't really want them to go to Hell. It just doesn't seem to make any sense."

"God doesn't expect us to understand everything that He does, Bertram, only to have faith in Him, to love and obey Him, and to love your neighbor as yourself."

"Maybe the reason we can't understand the things that God does sometimes is because sometimes He makes mistakes?"

"God doesn't make mistakes, Bertram. God is perfect. He is the Perfect Embodiment of Love."

"But how do we know that for sure? How do we know that He is perfect if He never tells us what He's doing? Maybe He makes mistakes all the time, and when He fixes them, we call them miracles?"

"We do know for sure that God is perfect, Bertram, because that's what the Bible tells us."

"That's what my mother used to say."

"And she was right."

"But God made people and people aren't perfect?" Bertram said.

"Yes. That's true. People are far from perfect."

"So maybe there are other things, besides people, that God made that are not perfect too?"

"Like what?"

"Like Heaven maybe?"

"Heaven?"

"Yes. Maybe that's the reason. Maybe God made Heaven too small and it got so crowded that not everyone could fit. But He wanted everyone to fit, only there wasn't enough room."

"Bertram, don't you think that God can make Heaven any size He wants, any time He wants?"

"Yes, I guess so, but maybe He doesn't want to make it bigger because He likes it the way it is. Maybe Heaven is like a perfect beautiful flower, and to change it in any way would make it less beautiful. So He keeps it the same size so that it stays perfect and beautiful, but then there's still that problem: where to put all of the new souls that are being made when people die? So, maybe God made a Second Heaven so they would have someplace to go, and just to be fair, He made it exactly like the first one, only a lot bigger, so that there'd always be room for everyone all the time, and everyone would be happy.

"Only they weren't happy," Bertram said. "Because even though the Second Heaven was just as good as the first one, no one really liked it because they didn't feel like it was the Real Heaven. It was just a copy of the real one, so they started finding fault with it and it got a bad reputation. They started calling it Hell and everyone began to say what a terrible place it was, when really, it was a very nice place, only no one believed it anymore.

"This upset God very much, of course," Bertram said, "because it made Him look bad. He'd never torture anyone for all eternity because He loves everyone, and to prove it, He sent some of His favorite angels there to live so they could see how nice it really was. Only the plan didn't work. The angels He sent there just got mad at Him because they thought they were being punished for no good reason and they had a big fight, but God still loves them. So maybe Hell isn't really such a bad place after all. That's why God sends so many people there, not to punish them, but because He loves them."

"Bertram," Jacob said, "people don't go to Hell because Heaven is too small. They go to Hell because they refuse to follow God's Word. Disobedience is a sin. Sin is evil and evil must be punished. Did your mother ever tell you that?"

"Yes, all the time."

"The truth, Bertram, is that Hell is a terrible place. It's meant to be terrible to punish those who disbelieve and refuse to follow God's Word. It is true that there are many things we do not know. Some things are a mystery and will always remain so, but there are some things that we do know. And one thing that we do know is that Hell is a bad place. It's a place you don't want to go to. It's a place filled with fire and brimstone, and the people who go there are tormented day and night by demons. They weep and gnash their teeth for all eternity. If you read your Bible, Bertram, you will see that Jesus made that point very clear."

Bertram thought about this and he quoted a verse that he knew from The Bible, something he had memorized from Romans, Chapter Eight. Bertram said, "Those who are led by the Spirit of God are children of God by the spirit of adoption, through which we cry, 'Abba, Father!'"

"That's very good, Bertram, where did you learn that?"

"In Sunday school."

"That's very good," Jacob said again, "but tell me, why did you say it?"

"Because God is like a father. And fathers get tried of explaining things to kids over and over again. And when they get tired, they just stop trying to explain it and let them believe whatever they want to believe if they ask too many questions. Maybe that's what happened with God. Maybe He just got tired of trying to convince everyone that the Second Heaven was just as nice as the first one, and so He just gave up trying and decided to let everyone believe what they wanted to believe?"

"No, Bertram, not God. What you say is sometimes true about some human fathers, but not about God, because God is not human. God is always there to listen to your questions and to help you find the answers."

"Oh," Bertram said.

"So you say you learned that verse in Sunday school?"

"Yes, I've been to lots of Sunday schools. We moved around a lot."

"You did?"

"Yes. We were always moving, but no matter where we went, we always went to church every Sunday. And every Sunday they always gave us homework to do so that we could talk about it on the next Sunday, scriptures and stories to read, things like that, like they do at your church."

"That's very good, Bertram. Do you know any other verses?"

"Oh yes, I know lots of them. They used to give out prizes to the kids who knew the most verses. I know all the books in the Bible too," Bertram said, and he recited all of the books in both the Old and the New Testaments for his uncle.

"That's very good," Jacob said again.

"It's funny," Bertram said, "but I've noticed that most kids in most Sunday schools don't ever seem to do their homework because they don't ever seem to know any of the answers to the questions that the teachers ask them. I think, maybe, it's because they know that they're not being graded, and so they don't think that it's important. I think, maybe, if churches started grading homework in Sunday schools and started failing kids when they can't answer the questions, then maybe more kids would do it."

"It's hard to say," Jacob said. "Children can be difficult at times."

Bertram agreed.

Jacob said, "I can tell that you are the kind of person who likes to learn things, Bertram. In fact, Mr. Sweeney tells me all the time how he wishes all the boys in his class studied as hard as you do, but I was wondering, Bertram, when you do your homework for your Sunday school lessons, do you ever pray about it while you're doing it?"

"No, I just study it the way I study the things I learn in regular school, like math and history. I don't pray about math or history either. I just study it and learn it."

"But you do pray about other things?"

"No, not usually."

"But you do sometimes?"

"I wrote a letter once."

"To whom?"

"To God, but He never answered it."

"What was in the letter?"

"I had questions."

"Like the kinds of questions that you're asking me now?"

"Yes."

"Then wouldn't you say that God has answered your letter after all? That's why you're here. God has sent you to live with me so that you can have your questions answered. You see Bertram? Everything that happens, happens for a reason."

"Oh," Bertram said quietly. "That's how it works?"

"Yes. Most of the time that's how it works. God uses men to do His Will."

"So He never talks out loud or writes letters back if you write Him?"

"Sometimes He does, but not usually, and when He does, He does so only to people who are very special."

"Like Saint Paul and Moses?"

"Yes."

"I see," Bertram said. "I think I understand it now."

"Are you sure?"

"Yes, I think so."

"Good. I'm glad, but if I may ask you a question this time," Jacob said. "What started you with all this thinking?"

"It was a story that we read in Sunday school last week," Bertram said. "It was about a boy who was born with only one foot and a crippled leg. The doctors told his mother that with an operation and a special foot that they could make for him out of plastic, that one day he might be able to walk without crutches. But the boy had bigger dreams than that! He told his mother that when he grew up he would be a world famous athlete and one day he would win The Boston Marathon!"

"And did he?"

"No," Bertram said. "He never did. He never won anything at all."

"Yes, that's true," Jacob said, "but he always finished all of the races that he started and he never came in last place, even against people with two good legs."

"You've read the story too!" Bertram was excited.

"Yes, I have."

"Then tell me, what does it mean?"

"I was hoping you might tell me."

"I'm not sure," Bertram said. "That's why I wanted to ask you. Everyone in the class seemed to think that the boy was a winner even though he never won a race. I understand that he did try very hard to win, but in the end he never did accomplish the things that he said he would do. He never won The Boston Marathon, and he never became a world famous athlete."

"He was famous to the people who knew him," Jacob said. "In life, we must be mindful that we are running the race that God has intended for us to run, not our own. Perhaps his gift was to inspire others to do better, not to win races with his legs and his feet, but to win races with his spirit. We must remember, Bertram, that it is the spiritual race that matters, not the physical one."

"Yes, but the spiritual race can be lost too."

"Yes, it can, Bertram."

"That's what made me wonder," Bertram said, "If one boy can be born in such a way that he can never win a physical race, then couldn't another boy be born in such a way that he can never win the spiritual one?"

"I'm not sure I understand what you mean. What kind of way?"

"Maybe he was born with something missing too, like the boy in the story. Only the something that was missing was something that you couldn't see."

"What kind of something?"

"I'm not sure, but I was thinking..."

"Yes?"

"If one boy can be born with something missing from his leg, like a foot, then maybe another can be born with something missing from his brain, something that keeps him from being able to believe in things that he can't see?"

"Something like what?"

"Like faith maybe?"

"All men have faith, Bertram."

"Are you sure?"

"Yes, because the Bible says it."

"But faith is invisible. How can you be sure it's there, if you can't see it?"

"Because faith is the only path to Salvation. Without it, we cannot know Jesus as our Savior, and without Jesus, we cannot be saved. God would never force us to run a race that we could never win, and then punish us afterwards for losing it. That would be the act of a cruel and despicable god. And God is not like that. He is loving and just. He would never do such a thing."

"So maybe God didn't mean for it to happen? Maybe it was an accident, like a boy being born without a foot. Sometimes things go wrong like that and accidents happen. Maybe that's why some people are good and some are evil, or why some people can believe in God and others cannot. Maybe it's because they're born with souls that are deformed?"

"Bertram, it is true that some people are born with more faith than others, but God always gives us the exact measure of faith that we need to find a path to Him."

"So all people have faith?"

"Yes. What they choose to do with it is up to them."

"Think soberly, each according to the measure of faith that God has given you," Bertram said. It was a quote that he had memorized from the book of Romans in the New Testament of the Bible.

Jacob said, "Yes, that's it exactly. You see? You already knew the answer yourself; you just needed a little help in seeing it."

"There are no accidents. Everything that happens, happens for a reason," Bertram said, though he didn't really believe it, but he felt that it was what his uncle was waiting to hear him say, and so he said it. And feeling that there was nothing left to be said on the matter, Bertram told his uncle that it was getting late and that he really needed to finish his homework for school tomorrow.

Jacob looked at his watch. "Oh my, it is late," he said. "Sorry to have kept you out for so long."

"That's okay. I learned a lot," Bertram said.

"Good night, Bertram."

"Good night, Uncle."

Bertram had his hand on the latch of the screen door and was just about to pull it open to go inside, when his uncle called his name again.

Bertram stopped.

"Yes Uncle?" he said.

"Bertram, I have a question for you now, if you don't mind?"

"I don't mind."

"Bertram?"

"Yes Uncle?"

"Bertram, are you saved?"

"Yes, I am," Bertram lied. It was an easy lie to tell because he had been telling his mother this same lie for many years and he was very good at it.

Upon hearing the lie, Jacob said the very same thing to Bertram that Bertram's mother would say to him. Jacob said, "Good, I'm glad to hear that." But then Jacob went on to say something very different afterwards, something that his mother had never told him.

Jacob said, "You know Bertram, even people who are saved, can still wonder about things. I wonder about things too, sometimes.

"And it's good to try to figure things out," Jacob said, "but we should never allow our desire for knowledge to cause us to question our faith in God. God gave us the ability to reason and the desire to seek knowledge. These are both gifts. God wants us to use these gifts in such a way so as to strengthen our faith in Him, but The Devil tries to take these gifts that God has given to us and subvert them. He tries to tempt us into using reason and knowledge to turn us away from God."

"Yes, that makes sense," Bertram said. "The Devil is pretty crafty. That's what my mother always used to say."

"I'm glad you understand that. Most people, some of them very good Christian people, don't seem to realize just how dangerous The Devil is."

"I do," Bertram said. "My mother used to tell me about it all the time."

"Your mother is a very wise woman."

"Yes, she is," Bertram said. "Thank you."

"Good night Bertram—Oh and Bertram..."

"Yes?"

"If you ever happen to have another question that you're wondering about, please feel free to ask me anything you want, anytime you want—only I would like to ask one favor of you."

"What's that?"

"I would like to ask that you not discuss any of the things that we talk about with your Aunt Elizabeth."

"Why?"

"Oh it's nothing serious. She's just very concerned about you and I'm afraid that it might cause her to worry needlessly."

Bertram smiled. "Yes, I think that's probably true. My mother is the same way. Aunt Elizabeth reminds me a lot of her. I like her."

"She likes you too."

EVIL CATERPILLARS AND PEOPLE WHO NEVER BECOME BUTTERFLIES

Life is inherently unfair. This is self-evident. Not all caterpillars live to become butterflies. Some are eaten by birds. Some die of starvation or disease. Some are born with deformities and lack the ability to transform themselves. Some die in the cocoon and never emerge. They never achieve fruition. This is sad and regrettable, but is it evil? And if it is evil, who is to blame? Is a person who never achieves moral fruition any more evil than a caterpillar that never becomes a butterfly? And when a person is judged to be evil, why must he be tortured in Hell for all eternity? Why can't he just be locked away without having to be made to suffer?

To the Faithless and the Unbelieving BERTRAM GREY

—Commentary from The Gospel according to Bertram,
Book One, Chapter Two—

When Elizabeth opened the screen door to the front porch, Jacob was sitting on the porch swing by himself. She walked to the swing, sat beside him, and snuggled up close. He put his arm around her shoulder. They watched the sunset fade from lavender to gray and listened to the crickets in the trees begin their nightly songs.

"Did you talk to him?" she said.
"Yes."
"How is he?"
"Oh, he's fine."
"So nothing's wrong?"
"No, nothing's wrong. He says he's just thinking."
"About what?"
"He has questions."
"What kind of questions?"
"You know, the usual questions that most boys his age have."
"About girls?"
"Something like that."
"Is he saved?" Elizabeth said.
"Yes, he is."
"How do you know?"
"I asked him."
"Oh, good. I'm glad. He's such a thoughtful little boy. I worry about him. It's a blessing that God has sent him to us."
"Yes, I was thinking the same thing," Jacob said.

CHAPTER 2

When Bertram Grey was fourteen he built ten white kites made of balsa wood and cheesecloth to fly at The Pietyville Annual Spring Picnic and Kite Festival. He won no prizes for them. That was not why he built them. He built them to answer a question.

Jacob saw Bertram with his kites and asked him what he was doing.

"It's an experiment," Bertram said. "I want to know why the sky is blue."

"With kites?" Jacob said.

"Yes. They're special kites. They're made of cheesecloth instead of paper."

"How do they work?"

"In school we learned that an object is blue because it reflects blue light. If that is true about objects, then it must also be true about the sky. There must be something up there that reflects blue light. The kites are my nets to catch whatever it is. Once enough of it has collected in the cheesecloth, it will begin to reflect blue light too, and the kites will turn blue, just like the sky. When that happens I'll bring the kites down to study them and see what it is."

"What do you think you'll find?"

"I don't know," Bertram said. "Blue dust, maybe?"

"Sounds like an interesting test," Jacob said. "Let me know what happens."

Bertram said, "I will."

And Jacob left Bertram alone with his kites.

Bertram flew his kites all morning long, all through the afternoon and late into the evening, but they never turned the slightest shade of blue. And when the picnic was over and everyone was going home, and Bertram finally pulled his kites down from the sky, they were still as white as they had been when he first put them up into the air.

He was very disappointed, of course, but the next day he made an amazing discovery. When he examined his kites more closely in the light of day, he found that the cheesecloth had, indeed, captured something from the sky. Each kite was coated with a fine layer of dust! But the puzzling thing was that the dust was not blue.

It was yellow!

And that wasn't all. As he looked closer into the net-like fabric of his cheesecloth kites he saw that he had captured other things too. He saw tiny wriggling specks with colorless wings and even smaller flecks of others things that did not wriggle at all. He saw bits of grass and pieces of dead leaves. He saw ladybugs and feathers and dandelion seeds and mysterious flecks of other things that he could not identify. This piqued his interest. Perhaps the answer to the question that he sought was hidden there.

So he cut up the kites into small perfect squares and put them onto glass slides so that he could look at them under a microscope to see them even closer. This is what he found:

He found that the yellow dust was pollen, the wriggling things were gnats, and the mysterious flecks that had so piqued his interest were only chips of paint, bits of rust and sand, and smaller parts of larger things that had been ground to pieces by the wind. And he wondered, "Was it possible that these combinations of things floating in the air, reflecting light, were the things that were responsible for making the sky blue? Or was it something else in the air?" Bertram puzzled over this mystery for many days and, eventually, he did find an answer.

But it only led to another question.

COLORBLIND DOGS AND THE BIG BLUE SKY

"You've been very quiet lately," Jacob said. "Something on your mind?"

"Yes," Bertram said. "The sky."

"The sky?" Jacob said. Then he remembered. "Oh yes, your test with the kites. So what did you find?"

"I found that blue dust does not exist."

"How do you know?"

Bertram explained to Jacob what he'd seen when he cut up the kites and examined them under a microscope.

Jacob said, "I'm no scientist, Bertram, but isn't it possible that blue dust might still exist? And the only reason you can't see it, is because it's too small to be trapped by cheesecloth, or seen with your eyes, even under a microscope?"

"No. Blue dust does not exist. I know. I read it in a book."

"Oh," Jacob said. "What kind of book?"

"A science book in the library."

"What did the book say?"

"It said that light is made up of waves, like waves in the ocean washing over a rocky shore. The big waves, if they're big enough, can wash over the rocks and make it to the sandy beach on the other side, but the smaller waves can't. They splash against the rocks and spray up into the air and never make it to the beach.

"The book said that the sky is like that too. It said that the sky is like an ocean of waves, but the waves are made of light instead of water, and the atmosphere is like the shore, but instead of rocks on the shore, there is air.

"The big light waves, the red ones, can wash through the air in the atmosphere without any trouble, but the smaller waves, the blue ones, can't. They splash against the air in the atmosphere like the small ocean waves against the rocks on the shore. That's what makes the sky look blue.

"It's blue light waves splashing or scattering, that's what the book called it, scattering. It's blue light waves scattering against the air in the atmosphere. That's what makes it look blue. It has nothing to do with blue dust. In fact, the book said that dust floating in the air is what makes the sky look red. You know, like during a sunset."

"Yes, I've heard that too," Jacob said. "Well, it looks like you found your answer."

"I thought so too…at first," Bertram said, "but then I remembered something."

"What?"

"I remembered that dogs are colorblind."

"Well yes, I think I've heard that too," Jacob said. "But why would that matter?"

"Because when a dog looks up at the sky he sees it gray, and when a person looks up at the sky he sees it blue, which means that the sky isn't really blue at all. We only see it as blue. If our eyes had been made differently, then we might see it as red or green or even black maybe. So it seems to me that the real question is not, 'Why is the sky blue?' but 'Why do we see it as blue?' And the book didn't tell me that. It only told me *how* the sky is blue, not *why*. The why is still unanswered."

"I can think of an answer," Jacob said.

"What?"

"It's very simple," Jacob said. "God made us. He knew how colors would affect our emotions. He knew that the color blue would make us feel calm and thoughtful, and that the color red would make us feel angry and uneasy. Imagine what would have happened if God had chosen to make our eyes to see a red sky instead of a blue one?"

"Yes, I can see how that would be bad," Bertram said.

"Then you agree?"

"Yes, it makes perfect sense! Maybe that's why there's no life on Mars!"

"I'm not sure I know what you mean?"

"Maybe when God made the people on Mars, He made them to see a red sky instead of a blue one," Bertram said.

"But there aren't any people on Mars," Jacob said.

"No, not anymore. But maybe there used to be. Maybe Mars was God's first try. Maybe He put animals and plants and water on it too, just like He did on Earth. Only instead of making them see a blue sky, He made them see a red one!"

"Why would He do that?"

"Maybe red was God's favorite color and He wanted them to see it too? Of course, He knew it would affect their emotions because it affected His emotions. It made Him feel happy to see the color red, and so He thought that it would make them feel happy too. Only it didn't.

"Instead it caused them to become mean and angry all the time," Bertram said, "and they killed themselves and everything else on Mars in a big war. Since then, there's been no life on Mars. So when God made people the second time, here on Earth, with Adam and Eve, He made things different. He made them to see a blue sky instead of a red one to help make them be a little bit more calm...maybe."

"I think that story has one too many 'maybes' in it to be true," Jacob said. "First of all, the Bible says nothing about there being a second Adam and a second Eve, and second of all, in order for your idea to be true, you would first have to believe that God made a mistake, and as I've said before, God is perfect. He doesn't make mistakes. Remember?"

"Yes," Bertram said. "So maybe He did it on purpose?"

"Why would God make a planet and put people on it just to be destroyed?"

"I don't know," Bertram said. "That is a good question."

CHILD PROTECTION LAWS IN THE GARDEN OF EDEN

Don't we as adults have laws that require us to lock away guns and other dangerous things that might cause harm to our children? Shouldn't we expect the same of God? And yet, He placed a loaded gun in the middle of The Garden of Eden without offering Adam and Eve the same protection that we provide to our own children. Shouldn't we hold God to a higher moral standard than we hold ourselves?

In a mortal court, a parent found guilty of the same offense would surely be charged with neglect or, at the very least, child endangerment. But not God. Neglect implies an error in judgment and God never makes mistakes. God would never make a planet and put people on it just to be destroyed, and yet He did make a garden and put people in it, knowing that they would eat from a certain tree and die.

If He is capable of one act, then why not the other?

It is a question worth further study.

—Commentary from The Gospel According to Bertram,
Book I, Chapter 4—

OBEDIENT POTTERY AND THE SIXTH PLAGUE

In the Old Testament, in the book of Exodus, the Bible says that after the sixth plague, the Pharaoh's heart had changed and he was willing to let the Israelites go, but then later he recanted, not because he had changed his mind, but because God had changed it for him. It was God who hardened Pharaoh's heart after the Sixth Plague, and then sent down a Plague of Hail to punish him for it. It was God who hardened Pharaoh's heart a second time and then punished him with a Plague of Locusts, and a third time and punished him with a Plague of Darkness. This might, at first, seem unjust and unfair because we, as an enlightened people, like to believe that God has given us free will, but He hasn't, not to everyone. Only to some. Those without free will are simply tools, common pottery to be used by God as He sees fit so that He may enhance the quality of His more noble works.

Pharaoh was created as a tool, a molded pot, to teach the people of Israel (God's noblest work) a lesson. As God said to Moses concerning Pharaoh, "I have hardened his heart...so that I may perform these miraculous signs...that you may tell your children...and that you may know that I am The Lord." This was the purpose for which Pharaoh had been created, to show the world God's power so that His name might be proclaimed to all the Earth. Pharaoh never had a choice in the matter. Free will had been taken from him to fulfill a Greater Scheme.

The same was true of the Roman soldiers who killed Jesus Christ. Jesus had to die. He had to be sacrificed to God in order to save mankind from Original Sin. That was The Plan. That was God's Plan. But who would do the actual killing? Surely not the people of Israel. No, that dreaded task was left to be done by some lesser work of God, a more common piece of pottery molded to serve that purpose.

As Pharaoh, the Roman soldiers who crucified Christ had no choice in the matter either. Free will had been taken from them to satisfy God's Plan. Again this may seem unjust and unfair to people who believe in free will and justice. Even the Apostle Paul must have been disturbed by such Acts of God, and in trying to understand the Mind of God, offers the following explanation. The Apostle Paul said this: "Does not the potter have the right to make out of the same lump of clay some pottery for noble purposes and some for common use? Shall what is formed say to him who formed it, 'Why did you make me like this?'"

This is not a very comforting thought for those of us who happen to be common pots and not noble ones, but all is not lost. There is hope because the Apostle Paul also said this: "What then shall we say? Is God unjust? Not at all! For God says to Moses, 'I will have mercy on whom I have mercy, and I will have compassion, on whom I have compassion.'"

But what does this really mean?

THE MAN WHO TALKED BACK TO THE POTTER

—A story from the book, Sayings and Parables of Bertram Grey—

Johnny Claybourne died and went to Hell. This came as a big surprise to him because while he was alive he did not believe in Hell, but death was an excellent teacher and Johnny soon learned that believing or disbelieving in Hell in no way altered its existence. And so, there he was...dead and in Hell.

And Hell, as The Good Book will tell you, is a very bad place to be, but what made it even worse for Johnny was having to be there in the company of The Eternally Damned—The Eternally Damned, that wretched self-deprecating majority of doomed souls, whose single occupation was to gnash their teeth, scream and wail, and beg to God for mercy. It was the only thing they did, and they did it all the time, even when they were not being tortured by demons. It was this, the deafening pitch of their incessant lamentations, which Johnny found to be the most annoying thing about Hell, for it made trying to take a nap virtually impossible.

Johnny had no sympathy for them.

This was not to say that Johnny himself did not scream or gnash his teeth in pain from time to time. He did (he was in Hell, after all, and it did hurt), but he kept the outward displays of his torment to a minimum so as to maintain some semblance of dignity. This was important to Johnny because Johnny had a very low tolerance for self-pity and a very high tolerance for pain, but more importantly, Johnny did not want to give "Anyone" watching him the satisfaction of seeing him suffer.

Now, the prospect of having to spend all eternity in so horrific and terrifying a place as Hell, would usually be enough to drive most any sane man mad, but not Johnny. No, Johnny was completely at ease with what was happening to him because Johnny knew that he was not Eternally Damned. Johnny was just in Hell for a visit. By the middle of next week, Johnny would be up in Heaven, learning to play the harp. Johnny knew this for a fact, not because Johnny had faith in some kind of Divine Justice. No, Johnny had something much better than faith.

Johnny had a plan.

In his Last Will and Testament, Johnny stipulated that his head be severed from his body immediately after his death and stored in a vat of liquid nitrogen for precisely one week, and after said week, that it be removed from the vat, attached to an electroencephalogram, ceremoniously immersed in a bowl of distilled water and thawed in the presence of a hundred different kinds of priests, monks, pastors, shamans, preachers, and witch doctors of every known religious order on the planet Earth.

This was done.

Johnny's head was revived and it lived for about four minutes, whereupon it suffered a massive cerebral hemorrhage, and died again—this time for good. Afterwards, Johnny went straight to Heaven, which caused a Great Commotion and a Universal Gnashing of Divine Teeth among all of the Angels and all of the Saints who greeted Johnny upon his arrival at The Pearly Gates. No one, it seemed, was very happy to see him there.

Johnny wondered why.

Gabriel explained it to him. "The problem, Mr. Claybourne," the Angel of God said to him, "is that you do not belong here. You belong in Hell."

All of the Saints agreed.

Saint Peter clarified the matter further. "Yes, Mr. Claybourne," Saint Peter said, "your presence in Heaven is an abomination. You have committed an unholy act that violates The Spirit of The Word Made Flesh. Gabriel speaks in truth. You do not belong here. You belong in Hell."

"I think you must be mistaken," Johnny said. "Before I died I accepted Jesus Christ as my Savior and was baptized in His name. I confessed my sins before men and vowed to live my life in His service."

"If this is true," Gabriel said, "then how did you come to find yourself burning in Hell?"

"Because the first time I died, I was not saved. I admit that. But the second time I died, I was. So here I am."

"Do you really think yourself saved, Mr. Claybourne, simply because you had your frozen and dismembered head placed into a bowl of water one week after your death? Is that what you honestly believe?"

"No," Johnny said. "Becoming saved requires something more. I know that. Having my head placed into a bowl of water only makes me baptized."

"If you believe that, Mr. Claybourne, then you are a fool!" John the Baptist said.

"Why?"

"Because you cannot be baptized after you are dead."

"Ah, but I was not dead," Johnny said. "I was alive. The readout from the electroencephalogram proves that."

"The scroll from this machine of yours? Is that what you are referring to? This machine you claim can write down the secret thoughts of your heart and mind?"

"Well no, it doesn't do that," Johnny said.

"Then what does it do?"

"It has many uses, actually, but primarily it's used to measure and to record electrical patterns from the brain to diagnose various brain disorders or, as in my case, to determine whether I was alive or dead."

"And it is by this machine that you claim yourself saved?"

"No, the machine did not save me. As I said, it simply measures and records patterns from the brain as it did when it was connected to my own severed head. It's these electrical patterns, made just prior to my second death that saved me, because they are my Confession and my Acceptance of Jesus Christ as my Savior."

"Your Acceptance of Jesus Christ as your Savior is invalid!" John the Baptist said.

"Again, I ask you why?"

"Have you forgotten? You had only your head baptized, not your entire body. Perhaps you forgot that little detail?"

"No, I did not forget it."

"Then what became of it, your body?"

"I'm not really sure. I willed it to science."

"And perhaps you will now try to convince us later that you had it baptized separately at another place?"

"No," Johnny said. "I don't think it matters."

"But it does matter, Mr. Claybourne. It matters a great deal. Jesus had his entire body baptized, not just his head. To even suggest that what you have done qualifies as a baptism only provides further proof of your heresy."

"Heresy?" Johnny said. "How does following the Scriptures make me a heretic? I thought believing was the only thing that was required to save a man's soul."

"Then you thought wrong, Mr. Claybourne. Even the demons in Hell believe in Christ, but they are not saved. Faith in Christ is more than just believing. It is about sincerity of heart and love for God. And your so-called 'salvation' had nothing to do with any of those things. You are trying to cheat your way into Heaven, Mr. Claybourne. You died just so you could peek at the answer, and once you knew the truth, revived yourself with a machine so that you could go back and accept Jesus Christ as your Savior!"

"Yes! That's exactly what I did," Johnny said. "Is that a crime?"

"It is a crime," John the Baptist said, "because righteousness from God comes only through *faith* in Jesus Christ to all who believe. God presented Jesus as a sacrifice of atonement through *faith* in his blood. You had no *faith* in Christ."

"I agree. The first time I died, I had no faith in Christ or God or anything else I could not see with my eyes or touch with my hands. I was born that way. God made me that way. Why should I be condemned by God when God made me like that?"

"Because," Saint Paul said, "The Potter has the right to make out of the same lump of clay some pottery for noble purposes and same for common use. The pot does not have the right to ask Him why!"

"I see. So I should accept God's will and burn in Hell forever so that He can use me as an example?"

"If that is God's will," Gabriel said. "So be it."

"But obviously that is not His will," Johnny said, "because if He had meant for me to be in Hell, then I would be there now. And I'm not. I'm here with you in Heaven."

"Lucifer was once in Heaven too," Gabriel said. "And shortly, you will again be joining him, but not by God's hand. Your own tongue will decide your fate."

"I don't believe in fate," Johnny said.

"Yes," said Gabriel, "There were a great many things you did not believe in while you were alive. Hell, as I recall, was one of them."

"I believe in it now."

"Only because you were there."

"Why should that matter? Don't the Scriptures say, 'For God so loved the world, that He gave His only begotten Son, that whosoever should believe in Him should not perish, but have everlasting life?' And I did. For the brief instant that my frozen head was thawed and brought back to life, I can assure you that I most certainly did believe in Christ, and everything else that was written in the Bible—I believed it all—from Heaven to Hell and everything else in-between—because, as you said, 'I was there!'"

"I have no doubt that you did believe," Gabriel said, "but the question remains: Was your belief born of faith or of science? Even you have testified that you believed in Christ only after you were able to prove by science that everything in the Bible was true. Grace is achieved, not by fact nor by science, but by faith. And by faith alone."

"What does that mean?" Johnny said. "That science is evil even if it helps a man to believe? Should a man stumble in the darkness, or should he light a candle so that he may see?"

"He should look to Jesus to light his way and he would have no need of candles!"

"Then using a candle is a sin?"

"I did not say that."

"If using a candle to see the world better is not a sin, then why is it a sin to use an electroencephalogram and medical science to see God better?"

"Because doing so demonstrates your lack of faith, Mr. Claybourne, and doubting is a sin. It is the greatest of all sins," Saint Paul said.

"You doubted too," Johnny said. "You did not believe that Jesus was the Son of God either. You spoke against Him and persecuted those who believed in Him. I don't see how I am any different than you are, except that when you doubted, God Himself blinded you and called you by name. It's easy to believe in God when He presents Himself in so conspicuous a manner. Unfortunately, I was never important enough to draw so esteemed an 'Audience,' but if I had, I would have believed too."

"Blasphemer!" Saint Paul said. "You and I, we are nothing alike. How can you claim to know anything about me or about what I believed? You who doubt everything and know nothing."

"I believe in the things I can see," Johnny said. "And for now, I see that I still remain in Heaven despite your heated objections, which must mean that God, who hears my every word, must also want me here."

"Yes," Saint Paul said, "that is true. You are here and the reason you remain here is no great mystery; you are here only that you may fall as Pharaoh fell, and in your falling glorify the Name of God and show to all Creation His Might and His Power. Your removal from Hell was not a vindication. It was an indictment, but you are so blind that you cannot see even that. Here you are in Heaven's Court standing without shame or humility, mocking God, perverting the meaning of His Word, and still you think you belong here?"

"Yes, I do belong here. I belong here because I have followed the Letter of the Law, and whether you choose to accept it or not, the Law gives me the right to be here."

"I might agree with you," Saint Paul said, "if you had kept to the Letter of the Law, but you have not!"

"I believe I have."

"Then you are in error."

"How so?"

"Through a flaw in your own twisted reasoning," Saint Paul said.

"Flaw? What flaw?"

"Is it not your own contention that the only outward display of your Confession to Christ before men is through this machine of yours? The one you say can record your thoughts and write them on a paper?" Saint Paul said.

"No, not thoughts. Patterns. It writes electrical patterns from the brain."

"Very well," Saint Paul said. "Electric patterns from the brain—patterns from *your* brain. Patterns you claim are your Confession to Christ?"

"Yes," Johnny said. "That is what I claim."

"Then we regret to inform you, Mr. Claybourne, we have seen these patterns, this thing of yours you call a confession, and it is our opinion that it is without meaning. It is nothing more than scribbled markings on scrolls of lined paper. You can claim it to mean anything you want it to mean. It is no more proof of your Acceptance of Jesus Christ as your Savior than a gypsy's testament that she is telling your future by looking at tea leaves!"

"God knows what was in my heart."

"How could that be? How could He know what was in your heart when you no longer had a heart with which to believe? It was no longer attached to your head! Is it not written: 'Confess with your mouth that Jesus is Lord, and believe in your *heart* that God raised Him from the dead and you will be saved?'"

Johnny smiled. "Now who's twisting God's Word?" he said. "Who can say where the heart of a man resides? Is it in the soul or is it in the body?"

"The fact remains, Mr. Claybourne—and the record shows—that after being revived, your frozen head died exactly three minutes and forty-seven seconds later."

"So?"

"So, Mr. Claybourne, even if we accept everything you have said thus far to be true—that you accepted Christ as your Savior, that you were baptized in His Name, that you vowed to turn away from sin and live your life in His Service—you did so with the knowledge that you would not live long enough to have the strength of your convictions tested. Such cynicism hardly seems the product of a sincere and honest heart, no matter where it may reside."

"Quite frankly, Sirs," Johnny said, "I wasn't sure how long I might live after I was brought back from death—an hour, a day, a hundred days—why should it matter? Don't the Scriptures say, 'The last will be first and the first will be last' and whether I labor in the vineyard for an entire day or but a single hour my reward shall be the same?"

"We are aware of what The Scriptures say," Saint Peter said. "You need not lecture us on it."

"Then perhaps I have misunderstood its meaning, since my guilt appears to have already been decided. Is this not a Court of Justice?"

"You keep forgetting, Mr. Claybourne, we are not responsible for your present dilemma. We did not send you to Hell. You sent yourself there," Gabriel said. "It was your choice not to believe."

"That's exactly the kind of thing I would expect to hear from someone who has never had a body," Johnny said. "Try being human for a while; it ain't that easy."

"But I have had a body," Saint Matthew said. "And even I must admit that your sincerity seems questionable. You have professed to believe in The One True God, and yet when you offered your Confession to Christ, you offered it in the presence of every kind of heathen idolater and pagan worshipper of false gods that you could gather together in one place. Why was that? Were you having trouble deciding who The One True God was?"

"Yes, I was. I never denied I had doubts. In fact, the first time I died I wasn't sure that any kind of god even existed, much less believing that there was one who was truer than the rest. So I invited them all just to make sure that whoever turned out to be The One True God was properly represented when I got back. It was a sin, of course, to doubt. I know that now, but I made that arrangement prior to accepting Jesus Christ as my Savior, so it shouldn't count against me. That is how it works, isn't it?"

"You walk a fine line, Mr. Claybourne."

"As for questioning the sincerity of my confession," Johnny said. "I have only this to say. I spent a week in Hell. Offering my confession to Christ was the most sincere act I'd ever done in my life, in both my lives."

"Even so," Saint Paul said, "your confession does not keep to the Letter of the Law, as you say, and so is rendered unacceptable."

"In what way?"

"You offered it not with your mouth, as the Scriptures say you must, but instead with the use of a machine."

"No," Johnny said. "I offered it with my brain with the use of a machine."

"I doubt if God will make a distinction between the two," Saint Peter said.

"Then by the Letter of the Law, anyone born mute can never enter the Kingdom of Heaven," Johnny said. "For how can he be saved if he is incapable of speaking the words of his Confession with his mouth?"

"He offers it with his hands," Saint Matthew said.

"Ah, an exception to the Law?"

"No, his hands become his mouth for it is with his hands that he speaks."

"Then I submit to you that my situation is no different. I could not offer my Confession with my mouth or my hands, and so, I offered it by the only means left to me, as a brainwave pattern transcribed on a strip of paper on an electroencephalogram. My brain became my mouth for it was with my brain that I spoke."

"That is different."

"How?"

"A person born mute suffers from a physical affliction that prevents him from confessing with his mouth. You were born whole. You had an opportunity to offer your Confession with your mouth, but did not take it, and now that you know the truth, you want a second chance."

"I disagree. No such opportunity existed for me either. I, as the person born mute, suffered from an affliction that prevented me from confessing with my mouth, or with any other part of my body for that matter!"

"What affliction?"

"I was born without faith."

"Faithlessness is not an affliction. It is a choice," Gabriel said.

"Again, that is your opinion. One that you are hardly qualified to make."

"It is no fault of mine that God made me an angel and you human."

"I agree. That is God's fault!"

"That kind of talk won't help your case, Mr. Claybourne."

"I don't need help," Johnny said. "I know my rights. I demand justice!"

These words, which sprang from Johnny's lips, reverberated across the Cosmos, rising up, falling down, striking out through time and space, until finally they touched the Ears of God. And God, upon hearing these words, appeared as a Whirlwind of Fire and took Johnny away to be judged.

"Oh, arrogant man!" God said, His wrath blazing with the fires of a thousand suns. "I have seen what you have done and I have heard the words that you have spoken against Me. Do you not fear Me? I am God Almighty! I could destroy you so completely that not one trace of your existence would remain in the minds of men!"

"Yes, I know that," Johnny said. "But destroying me won't solve your problem. I am the least of your worries."

The quiet in Johnny's voice caught the attention of The Almighty and He said, "Of what do you speak?"

"I am just one man," Johnny said, "but soon, others will follow, in ever increasing numbers. Men like me who aren't content with worship and blind faith; men who are driven by a desire for truth; men who will not believe in anything that cannot be proven and tested—anything—including You."

"Yes, you could destroy me now," Johnny said, "but that won't stop them from their progress. They will continue their research. They will build better machines. They will perfect their medical procedures and their knowledge of the human body, until one day a man will stand before you to be judged, a man very much like myself, but with one important difference. He will have been brought back from death whole. He will have spoken his Confession with his mouth and his body intact. What will you do then? What will you do when the race of men no longer have a need for faith because they can *know* the truth?"

"The day that men lose faith is the day that the world will surely crumble away," God said.

"What purpose will faith serve when men can visit Heaven and Hell anytime they want and talk with the angels at their leisure?"

"Without faith, men cannot be saved," God said.

"Wasn't there a time long ago when men sacrificed the blood of animals in Your Name and You forgave them?"

"That time has passed away."

"Perhaps the time of faith has passed away as well? I entered Heaven on this day, not by an act of faith or by grace, but by fact and technology. I clawed and fought my way to this place. If I can do that now, on this day, what may men of the future do? Perhaps it is time for a new kind of Covenant between God and The Race of Men, one based on something other than blood or faith, one based on something better, something that honors both God and Man—a mutual respect and compassion for each other, perhaps?"

"You are a fool," God said. "The race of men is a rebellious and stiff-necked people! They know nothing of honor or respect! It is impossible to teach them! I have tried! Better that they be wiped from the face of the Earth!"

Johnny said, "Would You sweep away all the people of the Earth, the righteous with the wicked? What if there were fifty righteous people in the world? Will You really sweep them away and not spare the place for the sake of the fifty righteous people in it? Far be it from You to do such a thing—to kill the righteous with the wicked, treating the righteous and the wicked alike. Far be it from You! Will not the Judge of all the Earth do what is right?"

And suddenly, God's anger cooled, for He had heard these words before. They were the same words that Abraham had spoken to Him on the day that He sought to destroy all of Sodom and Gomorrah without a thought to the righteous. On that day, God had listened to Abraham and had spared the righteous.

Perhaps it was time to listen again.

God said, "I see that you are a man who openly speaks his mind. Your point is taken. I will not wipe the race of men from the face of the Earth. But perhaps it is time that I let them go on without Me for they are a stiff-necked people and I might destroy them on the way."

"What will they do without you? You created them."

"They will make due. They can go their own way."

"Perhaps there is something else You might do?" Johnny said.

"I could confound their minds and scatter their numbers across the infinite span of the universe," God said.

"Yes, You could, but thousands of years ago you scattered them across the face of the Earth and look where You are today. What might happen a thousand years from today should you scatter them even further?"

"That is something to think about," God said.

Johnny said, "You are God. You can do whatever you wish. You can offer forgiveness in exchange for blood or for faith or for whatever you wish; that is Your choice. You are The Creator, Abba, The Father of All Things. 'You can have compassion on whom you have compassion and you can have mercy on whom you have mercy.'"

"Yes," God said. "It is as you say."

"But you are right. The race of men can be a stiff-necked people—or better—a steadfast people. They are steadfast in their desire for justice and for truth. And they are far from perfect. That is why they need You, to teach them how to use their new found knowledge with a moral and responsible hand. Perhaps this is the start of a New Age for God and the Race of Men.

"They are just beginning to grow in new and different ways, as they always have, recklessly and without fear. They will need Your guidance and Your acceptance if they are to succeed. They are Your people. You created them. You cannot abandon them now. Will not the Judge of all the Earth do what is right?"

"For the sake of the race of men," God said, "I will consider what you have said."

"Thank you," Johnny said, "and now I await your Judgment."

God looked down upon the tiny human called Johnny Claybourne and He said, "You are a man of action, Johnny Claybourne; a man to watch."

"Am I?" Johnny said.

"Yes. And I have been watching. I have seen the game you play with yourself when you are alone. The one you carry with you in a box."

"It is called chess," Johnny said.

"Yes, I know of it. It is a game for two opponents, is it not? Yet you always play it alone."

"I play against myself because I have not found anyone challenging enough to make the game entertaining."

God laughed. "Perhaps I should try you in a game," He said.

"I would like that," Johnny said. "We could talk."

So they set up the board and they made their moves. They talked about life and they talked about death and they talked about the nature of good and evil. God won the first game, but Johnny won the next two. And as they gathered the pieces together, and one by one placed them on the board to start another game, Johnny said to God, "If I may be so bold as to ask, and I'm sure there is a reasonable explanation, but regarding those souls now burning in Hell, I have often wondered this: What is the purpose of eternal torment without a means of redemption?"

Johnny never did know how to quit when he was ahead.

CHAPTER 3

God did speak out loud from time to time, though it was rare, and when He did speak in this manner, it was only to very special people. This was what Jacob had told Bertram. Bertram hoped one day to be special enough to have God speak out loud to him, that way he could know for certain if God really existed.

So whenever Bertram had a question, he always made it a point to ask God first, to see if he had become special enough to get a direct answer. And when God remained silent on the subject, as He always did, Bertram understood this to mean that he was still a little below the mark, and so he would have to find his Uncle Jacob and ask him instead.

"I have a question," Bertram said to Jacob on one such occasion.

"About what?" Jacob said.

"Is it true that all Catholics are going to Hell?"

Jacob laughed, "No, of course not. Where did you hear that?"

"Sarah told me." Sarah was the girl who sat next to Bertram at school.

"She did?" Jacob said.

"Yes, she said that Catholics don't get baptized the right way so they aren't really saved and so they all go to Hell."

"Did she say what way was the right way?" Jacob said.

"Yes, the way Jesus was baptized in the Bible."

"And how are Catholics baptized?"

"Sarah says they just pour a cup of water on their heads."

"Oh," Jacob said.

"Sarah says the Bible says that you have to be baptized just like Jesus was baptized or it doesn't count."

"I think Sarah is mistaken. The Bible doesn't say that, but Jesus did say this, 'I tell you the truth, unless a man is born of water and the Spirit, he cannot enter the Kingdom of God.' The Bible does not say how much water to use or how to use it. Only that a man must be born of both water and Spirit."

Bertram said, "But if Jesus was sent to show the way, then shouldn't we try to be as much like him as possible?"

"Yes, I think so too. But we must also remember what Paul said about judging other people. He said, 'Accept him whose faith is weak, without passing judgment on disputable matters.' What is the point of quibbling over the amount of water some people use in baptism? The fact that people are being baptized and living their lives for Christ is all that truly matters. It is not for us to pass judgment on our brothers. On the Day of Judgment God will look into our hearts and see what our true intentions are...to do His Will or to follow our own desires."

"But how can we be sure if we're doing the right thing if God is unclear about what He wants us to do? What if we think we understand what God wants us to do and later we find out that we're wrong?"

"There are only ever two choices in life, Bertram...to do good or to do evil. There are no in-betweens: If the thing you are doing glorifies God and inspires faith, then it is good. If it does not, then it is evil."

"Is asking questions about God evil?"

"Is that what Sarah told you?"

"Yes. She said that I was questioning God and that I was going to Hell. I told her that I was not questioning God, that I was asking questions *about* God. I told her that there was a difference."

"Well yes, I suppose there is, but you have to be careful about how you ask your questions, Bertram. Some people might misunderstand your intentions. Remember what Paul said to the Corinthians. He said, 'so whether you eat or drink or whatever you do, do it all for the glory of God. Do not cause anyone to stumble.'"

"To stumble? How?"

"By causing them to lose faith. Paul meant that we should never do or say anything that might cause someone to stumble and lose faith in God, because that is a sin. So if you think that your questions might cause someone who is weak of faith to question his own faith in God, then you should not ask it."

"Then Sarah was right?"

"Well no, you won't be going to Hell because you're saved. Right?"

"Yes. What I meant to say was, if a saved person asks questions about God because he wants to know more about God. Is that a sin?"

"Only if it causes someone to lose faith."

"Then I should not ask questions if I'm not sure?"

"Would that stop you from thinking about the questions and wondering what the answers are?"

"No," Bertram said.

"Then you should ask them...but only to me."

"Even if it causes you to stumble?"

Jacob smiled. He put a hand on Bertram's shoulder. "You don't have to worry about me, Bertram. You can ask me any question you want. My faith is unshakable. That's the reason God brought us together, remember? So that you could ask your questions and have them answered."

"And I won't cause you to stumble?"

"Never."

"Good," Bertram said and he asked Jacob another question.

THE SOLUBLE NATURE OF SIN

—From The Book, Sayings and Stories of Bertram Gray—

The Apostle Paul said:

One man's faith allows him to eat everything, but another man, whose faith is weak, eats only vegetables. One man considers one day more sacred than another; another man considers every day alike. Each one should be fully convinced in his own mind. The man who has doubts is condemned if he eats, because his eating is not from faith; and everything not from faith is sin. Do not destroy the work of God for the sake of food. All food is clean, but it is wrong for a man to eat anything that causes someone else to stumble. So whatever you believe about these things keep between yourself and God. Therefore let us stop passing judgment on one another. For the kingdom of God is not a matter of eating and drinking, but of righteousness, peace and joy in the Holy Spirit, because anyone who serves Christ in this way is pleasing to God and approved by men.

Bertram Grey said:

If one man is fully convinced that a cup of water will sufficiently cleanse a man's soul of sin and his belief is based on faith, then according to Paul's logic, this is pleasing to God. If another man is fully convinced that full submergence in water is required to cleanse a man's soul of sin and his belief is also based on faith, then according to Paul, this too is pleasing to God. But which man is right? Paul would have you believe that both men are right as long as each man believes sincerely by faith that what he is doing serves the Will of God and neither man judges the other. But is this true?

ARE SOULS MACHINE WASHABLE OR DRY CLEAN ONLY?

What is sin? Is it an actual substance composed of physical or spiritual matter, or is it merely an idea in the mind? What is immorality? Is it a physical or spiritual substance, or merely an idea in the mind? Is there a difference between the two?

There was once a time when only blood, from an animal sacrificed to God, could remove the stain of sin from the soul. This fact seems to indicate that sin is an actual substance that attaches itself to the soul and must be physically or spiritually removed. Blood was a necessary detergent in the cleansing process.

This changed, however, with the death of Jesus Christ. With his death blood was no longer required. Now water combined with a new cleansing agent, the Holy Spirit, was capable of washing away sin. This is why the question concerning the amount of water used in baptism is important.

It is not a quibbling matter.

Consider: If water and Spirit are both required to remove the stain of sin from the soul, and only a small amount of water is used, the cleansing process may be incomplete. Only a portion of the soul may be cleansed. Those parts not touched by both water and Spirit may still remain stained with sin.

One of you might say, "Baptism is merely a symbolic ritual to demonstrate one's commitment to God. God could remove a man's sin without the use of water. He is God. He can do anything He wants."

But if this is so, then why was Jesus Christ's death necessary? This is an important question because it implies that God is not all-powerful. He must abide by certain spiritual laws, unknown to men, just as men must abide by certain physical laws such as gravity.

One of you might say, "This is preposterous. God controls all things." But is God also not an Artist? And when an artist chooses a medium to display his inner vision, is he not bound by the physical limitations of that medium? If an artist chooses paint, he must abide by the law that states "yellow mixed with blue makes the color green." If he chooses clay he must abide by the law that states "water makes clay soft and fire makes clay hard."

One of you might say, "But God makes up the law. He can cause yellow and green to make red. He can cause fire to make clay soft." And this is true. But if God changes the law, won't that cause his previous works of art to become changed in unpredictable ways, or worse, to become completely undone?

If baptism is purely symbolic, shouldn't God take this into consideration and allow people living in desert lands, where water is scare, to use smaller amounts? But if, on the other hand, water is a necessary component in the soul cleansing process, a single cup or a single drop may be incapable of properly cleansing the entire soul of all sin.

The water may be like a medicine. If too little is taken the disease still lives, though temporarily weakened, and may eventually come back to kill the person who was thought to be cured. This is an important issue.

Perhaps God should come down to Earth to clarify it.

CLARIFICATION

There is much pain and suffering in the world. This is largely the result of man misunderstanding The Word of God. God said, "Be tolerant of those who are weak of faith." And good Christian people slaughtered the American Indians and took away their land. God said, "Love your fellow man." And white Christian people made black Christian people sit at the back of the bus. It is easy to understand how good Christian people can become so confused about what God is trying to tell them when God speaks to them in such riddles.

One day, God decided that it was time to put an end to the confusion, but knowing the unpredictable nature of man, He was not quite certain how to go about doing it without making matters worse.

The solution to His problem came to Him unexpectedly one day while He was working as a merchant marine out of Blount Island off the East Coast of Northern Florida. God overheard a comment made by a foreman speaking to his supervisor about one of his workers.

The foreman said: "Yeah, the guy's a real screw-up. I could throw him naked into a round room without any doors or windows, give him two solid steel ball bearings to look after, and before the day was through, he'd have broken one of the bearings and lost the other!" God thought this to be a very funny joke, and it gave Him an idea.

Man's confusion, God decided, had been partly His own fault. God had given man too much information and it had muddled his thinking. This time, God decided that when He talked to man again, He would make His message so simple and His presentation so direct that it would be impossible for anyone to screw-up its meaning.

In the past, God had appeared to the people of Israel as a Pillar of Fire and as a Pillar of Cloud. This too, God admitted, had been a definite source of confusion. Fire and cloud were complete opposites.

So this time, God decided that when He spoke to man again, He would appear to him as but one thing. He would descend from the Heavens as a Steel Ball Bearing measuring exactly one mile across, so that from whatever angle He might be viewed, He would appear exactly the same. And as He descended to the Earth He would issue forth a single message to all the people of the world in a language that all could understand. The message would be this, "Love your fellow man as you would love Me."

It was so simple an idea that God wondered why He hadn't thought of it sooner, and His heart welled with sorrow for all the needless pain and horror that had occurred throughout the ages because of His miscommunications. But He consoled Himself with the certainty that the future would be different, that man would finally desire to live in peace with his brothers, because man would finally understand that this was what God had really wanted from him all along. This time there would be no confusion.

So God descended from the heavens as a Steel Ball Bearing with His one simple message, "Love your fellow man as you would love Me," and God saw that man did listen. And God saw that it was good...but this was only the first day. On the second day however, man started asking questions.

"What did you see?" said one man to another.

"God is a bearing made of solid steel," said the other.

"No, God is silver," said another.

"God is made of chrome."

"God is a Great Circle," said someone else.

"He is a sphere."

"He is an infinite line turning on itself."

A great flood of opinion concerning God overtook the world.

"God is a round ball," someone said.

"God is a star," said others.

"God is light."

"God is a bright shining orb!"

"Lucifer shone brightly too!" cautioned the clergy. "That is what the name means, 'The Shining One.'"

"Yes," said the congregation, "that is true."

"This thing we saw up in the sky could not have been God," said the clergy. "God is a either a Pillar of Fire or a Pillar of Cloud. God is not a round ball."

"But why would Lucifer tell us to love one another and God?" said a child.

"To trick us. We should love God first and then our brothers. The shining orb told us to love one another first, and then God. That proves it was Satan!"

"It was God," said the child.

"No, it was Satan!"

Some people believed the child. "It was God!" they said.

Some people believed it was Satan. Two factions quickly formed and a Great War ensued to decide the matter. They fought each other until everything on Earth was destroyed and everyone in it was dead. And God looked down from Heaven upon the Earth and He saw that there was finally peace and He noticed how quiet and restful The Universe was without man in it.

And God saw that it was good.

CHAPTER 4

Bertram brought home his first straight "A" report card during the first semester of his sophomore year in high school because Billy was no longer living at home. Having graduated the previous year, Billy joined The Army and was now stationed in Europe.

Bertram felt that Billy's departure from the house released him from his moral obligation of keeping his grades low to prevent injuring Billy's self-esteem and embarrassing him in front of his parents. With this obligation paid in good conscience, Bertram felt freed to gain the recognition for the high grades that he knew he had always been capable of earning, but had never allowed himself to receive.

Bertram sought this recognition, not as a matter of arrogant pride or self-righteous justification, but as a matter of necessity. Bertram intended to go to college when he graduated from high school and he knew that his uncle and his aunt could not afford to send him; he did not expect them to.

They had already given him more than he could ever repay, and so, it was by gaining recognition for his work at school and earning a high grade point average that Bertram hoped to win an academic scholarship to any good college that would have him. But there was a problem with his plan, one he hadn't thought of, until he stood there with the report card in his hands, looking at what he had done.

Prior to high school, Bertram had never made any grade higher than a "C" because Billy had never made any grade higher than a "B" (except for Physical Education). And now, Bertram worried that bringing home a report card with nothing in it but "A's" might cause Jacob to suspect what Bertram had been doing all these years—purposely keeping his own grades low to make Billy's grades look better.

Bertram wondered what he should do.

At first, he considered trying to change some of the "A's" into "B's," but after a few practice attempts on scrap paper, he gave up on the idea. The alphabet, it seemed, was inherently designed for a person to cheat-up for higher grades, not to cheat-down for lower ones—a "D" or an "F" could so easily be changed into a "B," more so than could an "A" be changed into a "C" or a "D." Because of this flaw in the alphabetic grading system, Bertram was sure that Jacob would notice any alterations that Bertram might try to make to his grades, and so, in the end, Bertram decided to leave the report card as it was and to hope for the best.

Luckily, Bertram's fears were unfounded.

Jacob merely applauded Bertram for his hard work and his Aunt Elizabeth baked a chocolate cake to celebrate. Jacob said, "We always knew you would do well. It just goes to show you what hard work and faith in God can do!"

"We never stopped praying for you," Elizabeth said.

"Thank you," Bertram said.

"You should be very proud about what you have accomplished," Jacob said. "You've earned it, though I am surprised that you're not a little more excited about it!"

"I am excited," Bertram said. "I'm just a little tired, that's all."

"I'm sure you must be," Elizabeth said. "You've worked very hard all these years. I remember all the times Billy would be outside playing with his friends while you were inside struggling with your schoolwork. It must have been frustrating to see how easy it was for Billy to do so well in school when you had to work so hard at it."

"It wasn't so bad," Bertram said.

"You should be very proud," Jacob said again.

"I am," Bertram said and he asked for another piece of cake, not because he wanted one, but because he wanted to divert their attention from the report card to the cake. "This cake is soooo good, Auntie Liz. It's the best ever!"

"I'm so glad you like it."

"Could I have another piece?"

Elizabeth, happy to please him, promptly cut him an extra thick slice and put it on his plate. "You may have all the cake you want," she said. "I baked it just for you. You are the guest of honor!"

"Thank you," Bertram said again and he swallowed another mouthful of cake.

"Would you like some more ice cream with that?" she said.

"Yes please!" Bertram said. "Two scoops!"

"My, I've never seen you eat so much cake and ice cream before," Elizabeth said. "Didn't you have enough dinner tonight?"

"It's a special occasion," Bertram said, and raising his fork he stuffed another piece of cake into his mouth. He did not tell his Aunt Elizabeth or his Uncle Jacob the true reason his grades had improved so dramatically, nor would he ever tell them, because there was just no good reason for them to know. It was best to let them be happy celebrating his success, believing that they understood what they thought to be true.

Watching them in their happiness made Bertram feel a little sad for some reason. Perhaps it was because he felt as if he was deceiving them in some way, which caused him to wonder how many other little things that people believed as true and taught their children as true, but were not really true at all? Especially those things that they taught their children about God, such things as his own mother had tried to teach to him.

One such "truth" that had been taught to Bertram by his own mother and by the Sunday school teachers at church was the answer to the following question: "How can a loving and caring God allow bad things to happen to good people?"

The answers that Bertram had been taught were as follows:

1) God is testing our faith.

2) It is not God's fault. It is man's fault, because man brought sin into the world by disobeying God. So anything bad that happens to man has been brought about by his own hand.

3) Satan is the cause of all evil, but with enough faith in God, Satan's power can be rendered useless. Therefore anything bad that happens to man is, once again, man's own fault because man is weak of faith.

4) Free will. God gave man dominion over all things, including himself. Whatever happens to man, whether good or bad, is entirely up to man.
    a) But what about floods, plagues, hailstorms, and earthquakes?
    b) See: Reason 3) above.
    c) But then why do they call them Acts of God?
    d) Again, see: Reason 3) above.

None of these reasons ever satisfied Bertram Grey. He felt that there must be a better answer to the question of why bad things happened to good people, and he sought to find one. And he did find one. It came to him suddenly one day, not in a vision, but in a television, via a commercial advertisement for Slippery Dan's Quick Lube Ten Minute Oil Change. Sometimes, Bertram found that the truth, like God, also presented itself in strange and mysterious ways.

SLIPPERY DAN
AND
THE COSMIC OIL CHANGE

Slippery Dan says, "Change the oil in your car every three months or every three thousand miles. Not doing so is an immoral act for it allows evil to flourish in the world. It also reduces the life of your engine." Of course this isn't exactly what Slippery Dan said, but it's what Bertram thought about when he saw the commercials on television or heard them on the radio, which made Bertram wonder if the universe might not be like an engine too...a Cosmic Engine. And if the universe was like an engine, Bertram wondered how you went about trying to change the oil?

Bertram wasn't sure.

But he had an idea.

THE COSMIC ENGINE

Consider the Universe as a Cosmic Engine. Like our own Universe, it occupies all known space and time; it contains all known matter. The Cosmic Engine is the Universe and the Universe is the Cosmic Engine. Just as stars and solar systems and galaxies spin and whirl within our own Universe, timing chains and camshafts and motors spin and whirl within the Cosmic Engine. It is a perfectly designed machine, perfectly constructed and perfectly timed to run in a state of perfection forever, but because it exists in the physical world, this is not possible. It is not possible because there is a problem with reality.

The problem is friction.

As the Cosmic Engine runs in the physical, real world, it chaffs internally against itself due to friction. This chaffing process produces small particles of metal that must be removed and isolated from the rest of the engine to prevent them from collecting in critical areas causing the engine to become damaged over time.

Oil circulating within the Cosmic Engine serves this purpose. The oil cools the engine and continuously flushes away these particles. The particles are collected and isolated from the rest of the engine in a filter, in much the same way as degenerates and criminals are collected and isolated from the general populous by putting them in prisons to prevent them from causing damage to society.

The question is: Are these particles of metal evil?

The answer is: That depends on your mechanic.

Suppose you believe that such a thing as a universe or a Cosmic Engine can suddenly spring into existence by random chance. No engineer thought it up. No technician built it. No mechanic exists to admire its beauty or to curse its inadequacies, or to change its oil every three months or every three thousand miles. What would happen to such an engine? Inevitably, such an engine is doomed to self-destruction.

This is how: The small particles of metal that are continually being flushed from the engine and collected in the oil filter will steadily grow in number as the engine continues to run. This process will go on until the filter becomes so clogged with particles that oil can no longer pass through it. Once this happens, oil flow to the engine is lost. Cooling and lubrication is lost. The engine overheats. Internal parts melt and burn. The engine seizes. And everything stops.

But again, is this good or is this evil?

Without a mechanic it is neither.

It is the mechanic who determines what is good and what is evil.

If the mechanic finds satisfaction in the movements of the Cosmic Engine, he will want to see it continue to run. Anything that is beneficial to the operation of the engine will be considered moral and good. Anything that is detrimental to its operation will be considered immoral and evil. And therein lies the rub. The engine, which is good in the eyes of the mechanic, through its very operation, destroys itself by converting its own substance, a thing once considered good, into something that is detrimental to its own existence. Good has been directly transformed into evil because of friction.

We are an optimistic people. We like to believe that one day there will come a time when good can exist without evil. But is this possible? Or are the two forces inseparably joined? So that one cannot exist without the other? So that with every act of kindness and humanity we show one person, another is injured unintentionally and without our knowledge?

But God has knowledge of it.

Perhaps the physicist Sir Isaac Newton did too.

NEWTON'S THIRD LAW OF MOTION AND THE REASON THAT GOD ALLOWS EVIL TO FLOURISH IN THE WORLD

"To every action there is an equal and opposite reaction." This is Sir Isaac Newton's Third Law of Motion. Bertram studied it in his high school science class during the second semester of his sophomore year.

"Change your oil filter every time you change your oil." This is Slippery Dan's Second Law of Lubrication as proclaimed by television commercials and radio advertisements. Bertram learned of this too during his sophomore year in high school.

Though most people seemed to miss the deeper meaning behind Slippery Dan's television and radio prophecies, Bertram Grey understood them on a more philosophical level. He saw how they hinted at greater things, how they made subtle suggestions that spoke of universal implications far beyond the promise of a "ten percent discount if you mentioned this ad," and spoke of fundamental truths concerning the very fate of The Cosmos.

After all, an engine oil change was far more than simple routine preventive maintenance. It was an act of cleansing, a renewal, like a baptism. It implied that physical and spiritual perfection were possible, but only by the removal of that portion which caused the imperfection—be it damaging metal particles within an automobile engine or sin within the immortal soul of a man.

Although this was the same concept behind many of the teachings in the Bible and although it was the same message that his Uncle Jacob preached every Sunday in church, it was only after hearing Slippery Dan's version of it that Bertram began to question it's validity. If Slippery Dan was right, that meant that Bertram Grey had to be willing to believe that evil remained evil for all eternity—that it could never be redeemed. And Bertram wasn't quite sure if that was how the universe actually worked.

This distressing revelation came as a result of Slippery Dan's observation that the evil particles of metal within the engine, though washed away by oil, still remained intact; they were neither transformed nor destroyed, but continued to exist unchanged. Only now they existed in the oil filter rather than in the engine, and eventually would exist in a landfill or a dumpsite. This did not mean that they stopped being evil, because, although they were no longer a detriment to the automobile engine, they were now a detriment to a much larger World Engine, the Environment.

This fact worried Bertram and he wondered where sin must go when it was washed away from the soul of a man. Was it collected in some kind of spiritual oil filter for the universe? And when God changed this filter, from time to time, as He must, to keep the universe running smoothly, where did He dispose of it? In some kind of spiritual landfill, perhaps? Was this the true function of Hell, not to punish, but to act as a landfill for sin? And what happened when Hell became full? Or like our own landfills, would Hell just continue to grow larger and larger until, at last, there would be nothing left of the universe except Hell?

Bertram could not imagine that God (if He did exist) would allow such a thing to happen to the universe, which meant that Slippery Dan's insight, though intriguing, offered only a piece of the answer for which Bertram was searching. The implication that evil was created out of good and then became indestructible, was only half an answer, for if evil could be created from good, then why not good from evil? And if evil was indestructible and good could be created from it, then why shouldn't good be as indestructible as evil?

Newton's Third Law seemed to support this possibility, for it implied that physical existence, no matter how seemingly perfect, consisted of both good and evil in proportional and equal amounts. It had always been this way and it would always be this way because that was the nature of reality. Or to put it in Newtonian terms, "To every good, there is an evil." Which went on to explain a lot of things about God and why He did the things He did.

For one thing, it explained that God does not allow evil to flourish in the world. He is doing something about it all the time. It's just that every time God does a little good, He is also forced to do a little evil at the same time, and so most of the time it looks as if God is doing nothing at all. At first, this notion seems merely laughable and nonsensical. The contradiction is obvious. Why would God choose to do both good and evil at the same time, when God's true desire is to do only good? But there is a reason:

He has no choice.

GOD AS BALLOON ARTIST

Consider the universe as a fine work of art, sculptured entirely in rubber and air, created by God through the twisting and shaping of the length of a single multicolored sausage shaped latex balloon that expands into infinity. It is expertly manipulated and worked to form a universe complete with balloon clouds in balloon skies, balloon planets and balloon moons revolving around balloon suns. Some planets even contain balloon oceans and balloon forests with balloon people and balloon animals living in them.

Everything in this balloon universe is, as in our own universe, connected to everything else, because everything in it is made of the same stuff. A change in even the smallest part of this universe affects the universe as a whole because although the illusion of individuality exits, nothing really exists without being connected to some other part of the universe in some way. There are no islands, for even an island is connected to the mainland; you just can't see the connection because it is covered with water.

But God is a perfectionist, and even though His creation is beautiful and complete, He can't stop tinkering with it. He sees a flaw He hasn't noticed before—a small green forest, within a small blue planet, appears to be slightly over inflated. If He could somehow deflate this forest, ever so slightly, to make it perfect, then He could set down His tools and be satisfied with His creation and call the work truly finished.

But how to fix it?

The problem is not as easy as it first appears. He could carefully stick a pin into the forest and allow just enough air to escape until it is perfect, but then He would have to patch the hole and His work would be flawed in another way, or worse, if He is careless with the pin, the balloon forest may burst and be completely destroyed. So God decides that He must find another way. Using a pin is much too dangerous.

He could attempt to untie the balloon at one end and release air pressure that way, but then other parts of the universe would deflate in the process causing them to become imperfect. Returning them to their former states of perfection may prove difficult, if not impossible.

So God decides on the simplest of methods. He reaches out His hand and squeezes the balloon forest ever so gently until enough air is forced out of it and it becomes perfect, but the extra air forced from the forest has gone into the balloon planet's sun. Now the sun is too big. It shines too hotly. The balloon planet's oceans are boiling away. God squeezes the sun to bring it back to perfection and holds pressure on the forest, which still remains perfect, but the clouds get bigger and rain pours down from the skies and causes a flood.

He adjusts the clouds, but the moon grows in size and increases the actions of the tides. Beaches and shorelines are washed away into the seas. He adjusts the seas, while holding pressure on the moon and the sun and the clouds, but forgets to hold pressure on the forest, and once again the forest over inflates.

He is tempted to readjust the forest one last time to bring it back to perfection, but He notices that the universe is not as perfect as it once was. Many parts now sag because they were stretched beyond their normal limits during the previous adjustments, while other parts, like the forest, have become over inflated and bulge in odd ways. But overall, God sees that everything still works fairly well and if you view the universe from a distance, it still looks pretty good. Maybe He'll try again later.

For now, He needs a rest.

After all, it is the Sabbath.

THE LITTLE DUTCH BOY'S COUSIN

Most everyone is familiar with the famous story of Hans, the courageous little Dutch boy who saved his entire village by plugging a hole in a dike with his finger. What you are probably not aware of is the story of Hans' younger cousin, Harold, who one year later performs the very same act of selfless heroism, and yet receives neither praise nor admiration for his trouble.

Quite the contrary, all that Harold receives is a nineteen-count indictment for involuntary manslaughter, and although he is eventually acquitted of the charge, he and his family are forced to flee to America to avoid the persecution of angry villagers from neighboring towns.

If you are not familiar with the original story involving Hans, Harold's story is pretty much the same. Young Harold is journeying home one stormy night after visiting a friend when he chances upon a dike that has sprung a leak. He plugs the leak with his finger and calls out for help, but it is late and there is no one around to hear his cries.

Harold tries to patch the hole with rocks and twigs but nothing works, and he knows if he leaves before he can stop the leak completely that the hole will enlarge and the dike will burst before he can return with help. So Harold stays at the bottom of the dike with his finger in the hole, keeping his village safe, hoping that someone in the night might pass by and hear his cries for help.

But no one does.

It is a long, cold, rainy, and miserable night, but Harold never deserts his post and the village is saved. When dawn finally breaks and morning arrives, Harold sees the milkman and calls out to him. Harold tells the milkman the problem and the man returns to the village and brings back a crew of workmen to fix the leak.

All seems well, at first, and Harold receives a hero's welcome, until it is discovered that during the night the storm has caused two other dikes in neighboring villages to collapse. Nineteen people are drowned. The dike that Harold has saved is located along a stretch of largely uninhabited farmlands and no one would have died had it failed. Harold did not know this.

It is further discovered, after some analysis by Dutch engineers, that had this dike (the dike that Harold saved) failed first, it would have diverted stress from the remaining dikes in the system and the other two dikes, which are located in more populated areas, would have never collapsed. Harold is subsequently brought up on charges of involuntary manslaughter by the townsmen of the neighboring villages.

Fortunately, Harold has a good lawyer who points out that if Harold is found guilty of manslaughter, then Hans must be guilty of manslaughter as well, for Hans in saving the same dike a year earlier is responsible for weakening the dikes that failed in the most recent storm by forcing them to take up the added stress of the previous storm. Therefore it is Hans, and not Harold, who is really responsible for the tragedy.

The prosecuting attorney does not argue this point. He agrees that Hans' action of a year ago has very likely caused stress damage to the dikes in question and further submits that the stress of the recent storm would have probably caused them to collapse on their own anyway—had no action been taken.

And this is precisely the point, the prosecuting attorney contends, action *had* been taken—by God Himself. It was God who caused the dike that Harold saved to spring a leak in the first place, so that it *would* collapse harmlessly in the night, flooding uninhabited farmland, thus diverting stress from the two more critical dikes that did collapse. Ultimately, this is the greater crime of which Harold is accused, for in saving the dike that was leaking, Harold has interfered with an Act of God designed to save innocent human life, and in so doing, has caused the death of nineteen people.

But Harold's lawyer asserts that Hans is still the real killer and reminds the jury that even the prosecuting attorney's expert witness admits that Hans, in saving the dike during the first storm, has caused stress damage to the other two, which is why they failed during the most recent storm. Had Hans not saved the dike during the first storm, then these two more critical dikes would have never been catastrophically weakened, and Harold's selfless and heroic deed would have not resulted in disaster. But who is really to blame? Is it Hans or is it his cousin Harold?

The jury can't decide and Harold is eventually acquitted, but Harold and his family are still driven from the town by outraged family members of the victims who feel that Harold is an Instrument of The Devil. Hans and his family would have probably been driven from the town as well had they not all drowned six months earlier in a tragic boating accident—a fact not lost by Harold's lawyer who uses it to great effect during his closing statement to the jury, offering it as Divine Proof from God Himself that Hans is clearly the guilty party.

After the trial, a new law is passed proclaiming that small children should stop poking their fingers into places they do not belong and allow God to decide who lives and who dies, and everyone in the small village lives happily ever after, which just goes to prove the old adage that, "No good deed goes unpunished," a profound yet simple proverb that after closer inspection reveals itself to be nothing more than another variation of Sir Isaac Newton's most insightful and most illuminating Third Law of Motion.

LITTLE MIRACLES

The moral of both stories is, of course, that for every good action there is always an equal and opposite evil reaction, which is why it's so easy to screw things up with good intentions—and the more elaborate the intention, the greater the screw-up.

This is the reason that you never see God performing big flashy miracles the way He used to in the Old Testament. He has come to realize that the bigger the miracle, the bigger it's adverse effect on some other innocent part of the universe. But what happens when only a big miracle (like parting the Red Sea, for example) will get the job done? How can God save the world without destroying it at the same time?

Suppose God wants to stop World War III? How can He avert so concentrated and potent a force of evil as a worldwide war without the use of an equally potent and spectacular force of good, knowing that the use of such a force of good, will only, according to Newton's Third Law, trigger a second catastrophic event that is equally and oppositely opposed in nature to the very force of good that He used to stop the war? It would seem that The Hand of God is tied.

But there is a way.

THE PURPLE TOENAIL OF GOD

Instead of using one big miracle to stop World War III all at once, God uses a series of smaller concurrent miracles in rapid succession over a greater period of time to have the same effect and to minimize the adverse affects of His intervention.

If a billion people are to die in World War III, the deaths of these people will contain a finite and quantifiable amount of pain and suffering, and therefore, a finite and quantifiable amount of evil. Stubbing your toe against the leg of a coffee table as you stumble in the dark to go to the bathroom in the middle of the night also contains a finite and quantifiable amount of pain and suffering, and therefore, a finite and quantifiable amount of evil.

But the amount of evil contained in the deaths of a billion people is far greater than the amount of evil contained in a simple toe-stubbing incident on your way to the toilet. The ratio is perhaps trillions and trillions of times greater, maybe even more, but whatever the amount, it is a finite and measurable quantity, and once determined can be used by God to strike a balance between the forces of good and the forces of evil.

Let us say that this ratio, in its simplest form, turns out to be a million to one, that is, the evil contained in the death of one person during World War III is exactly equal to the evil contained in the unified act of a million people in the world stubbing their toes on coffee table legs all at the same time.

In practical application, this means that God can use His power to avert the death of one person during World War III (an act of good) and disperse the opposite effect of His intervention (an act of evil) through the unified stubbing of a million toes on coffee table legs (this, of course, does not take into account any variations in the concentration of evil should the person stubbing his or her toe swear at the moment of impact).

The problem is, obviously, that there are not enough toes and coffee table legs in the world to stop even a small war in this relatively painless and podalic manner. Stopping World War III would be a practical impossibility. The entire population of Earth would have to continuously stub their toes on coffee table legs for thirty-two and a half million years for such a thing to work. Fortunately, God has other options. The catch is, the more effective the option, the more painful the result to an unsuspecting world.

That is why there are still great tragedies in the world. That is why there are still airline crashes and highway fatalities and famine. That is why there are still hotel fires and senseless murders and hurricanes and cancer. These are all the little miracles that God uses to stop World War III or Armageddon or Asteroids from Space or some other Unforeseen Horror of which we are completely unaware from destroying the Earth and everything on it, especially us.

So the next time a church collapses and kills half the congregation, or someone you love dies in an airplane crash or contracts some awful incurable terminal illness, and you start to wonder, "Where is God?" Don't worry, He's out there and He's doing the best He can, and He's really sorry for all the trouble that you're going through, but there's not a whole lot He can do about it, because that's just the way the universe works.

So before you start feeling sorry for yourself and you start thinking that God has abandoned you, try to see it from His point of view the next time there is trouble in your life, and ask yourself this question instead, "Which would you rather have, World War III or cancer?"

THE FLOODGATES OF CREATION

You might think that there is a better way of controlling evil in the universe, but there isn't. Newton's Third Law won't allow it. It is an integral part of the way the universe is constructed and can't be changed without causing all of Creation to become undone. Balance must always be maintained. This is, in fact, God's major role in the universe, to regulate the flow of good and evil so that the balance is kept fair and equal. He is like a lever man on a dam, trying to control the force of a turbulent river.

But the flow of good and evil, like the force of a turbulent river, can be a tricky thing to manage, especially when the rainy seasons come and the floodwaters begin to rise. People will suffer no matter what decision the lever man makes.

If the lever man chooses to pull the lever shut to close off the floodgates to the dam, he will save all of the people downstream of the dam, but then the river will back up and flood everything upstream of the dam. Homes, crops, livestock, and human lives will be ruined.

Or, he could push the lever open and release the full fury of the river's force to the people below, washing away everyone and everything downstream of the dam to keep the people upstream of the dam safe from harm.

Either choice the lever man makes will cause suffering.

But if the lever man is fair and impartial, he will seek to find a balance, allowing for equal amounts of destruction on both sides of the dam, that is, if he is fair and impartial. But what if he is not? What if he is willing to accept bribes? Or worse, what if he is an opportunist and accepts bribes from both sides without having any intention of favoring one side over the other?

What would the people do when the floods came anyway? Would they blame the lever man and come to hate him, or would they blame themselves for not offering him enough money and praise? Bertram felt that God (again, if He existed) would be faced with similar problems, only on a much grander scale, because God was lever man to more than just a single dam; He was Lever Man to the Floodgates of All Creation. But what kind of Lever Man was He?

He did seem to accept bribes when they were offered in an appropriate manner, although they were not called bribes. They were called tithes. And He did seem to favor one group of people over another, so He wasn't completely impartial. The Jews were His Chosen People, the Bible said, which brought up another mystery that Bertram did not fully understand. If the Jewish people were God's favorites, then why did He always seem to treat them so badly?

All of these questions played in Bertram's mind for many days, so he read his Bible and he prayed for wisdom and he tried to think as little as possible, remembering a previous conversation with his uncle about studying too much and praying too little.

And God having heard Bertram's prayers, and having come to realize long ago that any answer He could give to Bertram would only result in three more new questions that would also require answering, did what He always did. He pretended not to hear, so that Bertram would have to ask his uncle.

Or at least that was how it seemed to Bertram.

CHAPTER 5

Bertram waited a day or two longer than usual before asking his uncle his next question, just in case God intended to answer Bertram more directly. But after a week's worth of waiting, Bertram felt that he had received an answer: he was still not quite special enough to have God talk to him out loud.

And so Bertram went to see his Uncle Jacob instead.

Jacob said, "What's your question?"

"It has to do with science," Bertram said, and he explained his Theory of Newton's Law and How It Affected God's Ability to Run the Universe. Jacob listened intently, and could tell from the start that the whole thing was just pure silliness.

But Jacob knew that things that seemed silly to adults were often times very serious to children, and so he decided to indulge his nephew's overactive imagination because it was late Friday, and Jacob was still struggling to finish his sermon for the Sunday service. Jacob hoped that by taking a short break from his work, it might help him to gain a fresh perspective.

"It sounds like you've put a lot of thought into this," Jacob said.

"And I prayed about it too," Bertram said.

"That is good. It's an interesting perspective, combining religion and science like that, but what's your question?"

"Do you think it might be true? You know, about Newton's Law and the Universe?"

"No."

"Why?"

"Because God only does good, not evil. All things of God are good. All things of Satan are evil. Remember?"

"But God made Satan."

"Yes."

"So doesn't that make Him partially responsible for what Satan does?"
"God made you too, didn't He?"
"Yes."
"If you decide to commit a crime, do you think that God should be held accountable for that too?"
"No."
"And why is that?"
"Because I have free will?"
"Yes. It's the same with Satan. God gave him free will too."
"But what about Newton's Law?" Bertram said.
"It still works. You just have to put it into a proper perspective. Newton says that to every action there is an opposite reaction. You say that to every good there is an evil. And that may or may not be true. But if it is, then God is responsible for the good part of the action and Satan is responsible for the evil part of the reaction. It's just that simple."
"Oh," Bertram said.
"What's wrong now?"
"Nothing, I was just wondering what the world must have been like before God created Newton's Law. If nothing can happen without causing the opposite to happen at the same time, I was wondering if the same might be true about good and evil. Could good have even existed before God created Satan?"
"Yes, it was called Paradise."
"But if God wanted to do evil without Satan, He could, couldn't He?"
"No, because God is perfect. He only does good."
"But what about what it says in First Samuel, Chapter Sixteen?"
"Oh, so you've been reading your Bible again? That's good."
"Yes, and I've been trying not to think as much."
Jacob said, "Have you now?"
"Yes, I've been praying too."
"Well I'm very glad to hear that, however, I'm afraid I'm not too familiar with that particular passage. What does it say?"
"It says, 'but the Spirit of the Lord departed from Saul, and an evil spirit from the Lord troubled him.'"
"Yes?"
"It sounds to me like God sent down an evil spirit to hurt Saul."
"I know it may seem that way, but I assure you, it is not. God does not do evil, though He can allow evil to happen through Divine Permission as He did with Job. When God withdraws His favor from a man, evil has an opportunity to take control. This doesn't mean that God has done the evil. He simply allows it to happen."
"I see. It's like if I see someone drowning and refuse to help him and he dies, then I'm not responsible for his death because I didn't actually kill him?"
"No, you are responsible, but that doesn't necessarily mean that allowing him to drown is an evil act. If the person drowning is a small child in a wading

pool and you allow him to die, that would be evil. But if the person who drowns is a criminal who is trying to run away from the police by swimming across a river, and he drowns because you decided not to help him, then depending on the circumstances, it may not be evil."

"How?"

"Well let's say that he didn't drown because you helped him and he managed to escape and wound up killing someone or committing another crime, then to my way of thinking, his death wouldn't be considered evil, because by his dying, the Devil could no longer use him to harm other people. But that's something only God can know. You, as a normal human being, cannot know what is in the heart and mind of another person. Only God can know that, so you must always strive to do good. That means if you ever do happen to see someone drowning, please, do try to save him."

Bertram laughed a little. "I will," he said.

"Good, now if that's all I can—"

"So even when God appears to be doing something wrong," Bertram interrupted, "He's really doing something good? We just can't see what it is?"

"Yes, that's a good way to put it, I guess."

"Like when He accepts bribes from people who want to gain His favor?"

"Bribes?"

"Isn't tithing like taking a bribe, giving money to God to gain His favor?"

"I think you're confused as to who is being bribed, Bertram. God sets forth rules for men to follow and if they follow them they will be rewarded. God is bribing man to do good works in His Name by promising him greater rewards in Heaven. God is bribing man, not the other way around, and I'm sure He wished He didn't have to do it, but sadly that's the way most people are. They need to know that they're going to get something in return before they help someone else."

"Yes, I've known people like that too," Bertram said.

"You can't gain God's favor just by giving Him money or things. It doesn't work that way. And it's a good thing too, because if that's all it took, then there'd be a lot of unhappy people in the world."

Bertram gave Jacob a questioning look.

"Ah, I see that you have another question, so let me answer this one before you ask it. You're probably thinking, 'Why would anyone be unhappy if they had God's favor?'"

Bertram nodded his head without saying, "Yes."

Jacob said, "The answer to that question is because once they get God's favor, they'd find out pretty quick that having it doesn't necessarily mean that they're going to get any special treatment, or rather, they will get special treatment, just not the kind of special treatment they expected, or even wanted."

Again, Bertram gave his uncle a questioning look.

"You see Bertram, gaining God's favor may mean that you get treated even worse than you did before. Look at the Israelites. They are The Chosen People and look at all the suffering they have had to endure."

"Yes, I've been wondering about that too."

"Being favored doesn't mean that you get a free ride into Heaven, Bertram. If anything, it may mean that it's even harder for you to get there. Finding favor with a person usually means that you expect more from that person. Look at how I treated Billy compared to how I treated you."

"Billy is your son, so of course you'll treat him...differently."

"No, that's not what I mean. Finding favor has nothing to do with blood. I love you and Billy equally, but I favor you more."

"You do?"

"Yes. When you first started living with us, I saw that you were more mature than Billy, even though you were a few years younger. And so I began to trust you more. And slowly, without realizing it, I began to find myself expecting more from you. I began to feel that I could always count on you to do what was right and good. I knew that I didn't have to keep an eye on you the way I did with Billy, which allowed me to spend more time with him, trying to encourage him to be a better person. So you see, Bertram, by gaining my favor you earned not only my trust, but also my neglect."

"I never felt neglected."

"Maybe neglect is too strong a word. I gave things to Billy that I didn't give to you. I paid him more attention."

"Because he's your son."

"Because he needed it. You didn't. Here's something I think may help you to understand," Jacob said. "It's a little thing, something I did for Billy when you were younger. I never told you about it because I didn't feel there was a need, but you're older now and I think you're mature enough to understand its meaning without being hurt by it."

"I won't be hurt," Bertram said.

"I know that now," Jacob said, "but when you first came to live with us I wasn't so sure, and then later, after Billy left, there just didn't seem to be any need in bringing it up. But now I think you can learn from it, so I'll tell you."

Bertram nodded that he understood and that he was willing to learn.

Jacob said, "It's really a very small thing. You might even think it silly, but back before you began to live with us, I used to pay Billy a small reward for every letter grade of 'C' or above that he earned on his report card. Billy never had much interest in school. God, it seemed, had chosen to give him less than the full measure of determination that he had given to you. By paying him, I hoped to motivate him to put more effort into his studies by giving his schoolwork a meaning that had value to him."

"Like the way God bribes men with Heavenly Rewards?"

"Yes, just like that. When you came to live with us, I intended to pay you just like I paid Billy, but when I told Billy of my intentions, I was surprised to see him become angry and sullen. I told him to shape up or I wouldn't pay him either, thinking that the threat might shock him into seeing how selfish he was being, but it didn't. He only became more hateful and defiant about it and he blamed you."

Jacob said, "I hadn't realized how much your living with us had affected him. We'd always taught Billy the importance of charity, but charity requires practice and I came to realize that I probably hadn't given him enough opportunities to practice it, so I decided to try and fix that. But after speaking with him at some length, I could see that Billy wasn't interested in fairness or in charity and that if I had taken a stand I would have only worsened the situation and further strengthened his resentment towards you.

"So I made a compromise with him," Jacob said. "I told him that I would continue to pay him as long as he promised to keep it a secret. That way I could be sure he would not risk losing the money by trying to taunt you with it. Later, I hoped to work on Billy's selfishness in private, and in ways that didn't put you in the middle."

"That's okay. I wouldn't have wanted the money anyway."

"I know, but if a parent is good, he tries to be fair and equal in the treatment of all the children under his care. Sometimes that's not always possible; some children need more attention and some need less. That's what I meant when I said that you had earned my neglect, because even though you were the better student and even though you were the more responsible person, it was Billy who seemed to get the reward. I gave him money. I gave him more of my time, but to you I gave nothing extra."

"I always got what I needed."

"And you never held any resentment in your heart," Jacob said. "I saw that, and that is why you earned my favor. God is no different. He is a good parent who is concerned for the welfare of all his children. He knows everything about us. He understands our strengths. He understands our shortcomings. And He acts accordingly, so that sometimes it seems as if He is giving more to the people who don't deserve it and less to the people who do."

"Yes," Bertram said, "I understand it now."

"Understand what?"

"Everything. It all makes sense now."

"I'm glad to hear that," Jacob said. "Anything else I can help you with?"

"No."

"Good. Now I'm a little rushed for time at the moment, so if you would kindly shut the door on your way out, I'd appreciate it."

"I'll lock it so no one will disturb you," Bertram said.

"That won't be necessary. Just close it. That will be fine."

"Okay," Bertram said. "Goodbye, Uncle. And thank you."

"You're welcome, Bertram," Jacob said, as he always said to his nephew after answering one of his questions, then he picked up a pencil and started back to work on his sermon, but something was blocking Jacob's thoughts, something that hadn't been said, but should have been. And at the risk of generating another question from Bertram, Jacob laid down his pencil and called out to his nephew.

"Yes, Uncle?"

"Bertram, there was something else I wanted to tell you."

"Yes?"

"I wanted to tell you that I love you as if you were my own son and that I am very proud of you."

"Yes," Bertram said. "I already knew that. You and Aunt Elizabeth show me that all the time."

"Well, I wanted you to hear it too. You are a good son and a fine person."

"And you are a good father," Bertram said.

"Thank you, Son. Believe it or not, grown-ups need to hear that too, every now and then. It helps us to know that we're on the right track."

"You're welcome," Bertram said.

"Oh, and Son—"

"Yes?"

"Maybe you should lock the door after all—maybe if I'm locked in, it will help to motivate my brain."

"But you won't really be locked in," Bertram said. "You can unlock the door any time you want."

"Yes, of course I can. I was just—"

In that instant, the perfect idea for a sermon formed in Jacob's mind. He pushed aside an old stack of papers, grabbed a fresh pencil and took a blank sheet from another stack. Then he began to furiously scribble out a sermon. Bertram was still at the door, holding the doorknob, awaiting further instructions. Jacob glanced up at him and said, "Lock the door and don't look back, Son. I think you may have just saved me!"

Bertram grinned and locked the door. He was just about to shut it when Jacob said, "Tell your mother that I'm not seeing any visitors until further notice, and anyone who disturbs me does so at their own peril—unless it's to tell me that supper is ready!"

"Yes, Father!" Bertram said. He pulled the door shut, bounded up the hallway and into the kitchen to see if his Aunt Elizabeth needed any help with supper.

CAIN AND ABEL AND THE CURSE OF BEING FAVORED

—From The Gospel according to Bertram, Book 1, Chapter 6—

Bertram had always been taught that God favored Abel's sacrifice over Cain's sacrifice, because God had favored Abel over Cain, but now Bertram saw that this interpretation was in error. "Being favored doesn't mean that you get the better treatment," Jacob had told him, and Bertram, now fully understanding this truth, saw that the same had been true of Cain. Why else would God have praised only Abel's offering, unless it was because God had seen that Abel required more time and more encouragement to be a better son, just as Billy had required more encouragement and praise from Jacob.

"It is love that I desire, not sacrifice," God had said through the Prophet Hosea.

As Bertram had done with his uncle, Cain had also done with God. Cain had won God's favor and His neglect, but Cain had not understood this. Cain saw only that he had not received the same amount of praise for his offering as his brother had, and so Cain became jealous of his brother and angry with God.

When God saw this, He was greatly distressed because He knew that Cain was the better man, which was why God went to Cain and He said, "Why are you angry? Why is your face downcast? If you do what is right, will you not be accepted? But if you do not do what is right, sin is crouching at your door; it desires to have you, but you must master it."

In saying these words to Cain, God was giving Cain the greater blessing, for God was acknowledging that Cain was no longer a child. Only children needed the praise and approval of their parents to encourage them to do what was right. Cain was a man now, and as a man was expected to master his emotions and to set the example for his younger brother. But Cain did not see how God was honoring him. Jealousy and anger overwhelmed him, and he killed his brother Abel.

There is another thing that Cain failed to see, that there can be a problem in knowing God too well. For in knowing God too well, we may draw His favor, and in drawing His favor we may increase His expectations of us. And Bertram, seeing this truth, saw also how it was the answer to the mystery of why God, out of necessity, was forced to pick a Chosen People among all the peoples of the Earth and why, once chosen, proceeded to treat them so badly.

God is forever bound to the principles of Newton's Third Law of Motion, which decrees that for every act of good there must be an equal and corresponding act of evil, and although God is capable of stopping bad things from happening to good people, he must be mindful about how He goes about doing it, for the two forces, good and evil, must forever be kept in balance.

Which brings us to the crux of the problem: What happens when the evil that must be counteracted is so great that God has exhausted all of the relatively harmless ways of dispersing the opposite effects of His interventions for good?

There must be a place that He knows He can visit these acts of evil without causing a resentment against Him that would permanently damage His relationship with man. He needs a man like Job, who understands that it is because God finds such greatness in him that he is made to suffer, but one man alone is not enough to bear all the burdens of the world upon his soul.

God needs a group of men—an army of Jobs, a Chosen Few—that He can trust to never hate Him, and to always understand that He loves them no matter what happens. Bertram, now fully understanding The Price of being

Chosen thought that, yes, perhaps The Israelites did deserve that free ride into Heaven. They had earned it. They were still earning it. They would go on earning it.

They would never know peace.

They could never know peace.

For God had found favor with them.

For the next eight and a half days, Bertram asked his uncle no questions, because his uncle had explained everything to him so completely that he had no questions to ask. Bertram understood now that God did not take bribes; it was God who bribed man. He understood that God did play favorites, but that didn't necessarily mean that you were getting the easy way out.

Most importantly of all, Bertram understood that God was perfect and could never commit an evil act because God was a source of goodness only. He was The Source of All Goodness. This explanation made perfect sense to Bertram and he was satisfied with all that had been revealed to him, but then came the ninth day, and on this day, this brief period of clarity ended.

It ended about the same time he had to do an oral report in his high school science class on the physicist, Albert Einstein and his famous Theory of Relative Simultaneity. But it wasn't Albert Einstein and his theory that had caused Bertram to lose clarity. It was a verse he had read in Leviticus in Sunday school where God said to Moses, "If anyone curses his God, he will be held responsible; anyone who blasphemes the name of The Lord must be put to death. The entire assembly must stone him. Whether an alien or native-born, when he blasphemes the Name, he must be put to death." This time it was God who caused Bertram to question.

Einstein, as did Newton, only suggested an answer.

The question was "Why would God want men to kill for Him when God could do the killing Himself?" God had killed men before and in great numbers in The Great Flood; at Sodom and Gomorrah; during the Passover; and during the Exodus from Egypt. Why stop now? There had to be a reason.

There was a reason.

The reason was Relative Simultaneity.

In fact, The Theory of Relative Simultaneity not only explained the reason God directed men to kill for Him, but it also explained another baffling mystery that had bothered Bertram for many years.

It explained:

THE REASON GOD THINGS HAPPEN TO BAD PEOPLE

Why does it seem as if some morally corrupt people have all the luck in the world? They have no sense of charity or of kindness, and really deserve only to be run over by a bus (preferably more than once). And yet these kinds of people seem to go through life without a care in the world.

Every good thing is laid at their feet and they only squander it on themselves without a thought to the less fortunate. How can God allow this to happen? The answer is Relative Simultaneity. But perhaps you have never heard of it because you were asleep when they talked about it in your high school physics class.

Relative Simultaneity, simply put, means that a person who is standing still will see a different reality than a person who is moving. Einstein's classic example of this strange fact is that of a person standing on a hill who sees two lightning bolts strike the ground at the same time, while a person riding on a train sees them strike separately, first one and then the other. And if the train happens to be traveling at the speed of light, the person on the train will only ever see one lightning bolt strike the ground!

If all this talk of relativity still has you confused, perhaps a short demonstrative tale might help to clear things up a bit. Consider then the story of the late and briefly famous, self-proclaimed ecclesiastical comedian, Orlan Fritz and his Most Exalted and Most Omnipotent Critic:

ORLAN FRITZ AND THE WRATH OF GOOD

God hates Orlan Fritz, and with good reason. The man simply isn't funny. But judge for yourself. Here is an excerpt from Orlan's most famous routine. The one that gets him killed...

ORLAN: No, I'm not saying that God is a woman. I'm saying that God has an ex-wife and she was awarded the Earth as part of their divorce settlement. Everyone knows that the ex-wife always gets the house!

(*Mingled laughter from the audience. Some light applause.*)

ORLAN: That's why we don't see God as often as we used to in The Old Testament. After the divorce she hit Him with a restraining order and now He can't come within twenty million miles of the Earth!

(*Orlan takes a sip of water from his glass.*)

ORLAN: So you see? There is no Satan; it's just God's ex-wife trying to make Him look bad by trashing the place!

(*Big laughs from all the men in the audience. The women elbow their husbands and boyfriends in the ribs.*)

ORLAN: Of course God sneaks in when she's not looking and tries to fix things, but He never has a chance to finish the job, and so the world remains in a general state of chaos.

(*More male laughter from the audience. The women boo and hiss.*)

ORLAN: But then again, I could be wrong. God could be a woman.

(*The women applaud.*)

ORLAN: I mean who else would have come up with the idea of circumcision? Surely not a man—but seriously, I wonder how God sprang that one on Abraham?

(*Orlan holds a white toupee to his chin to play the role of God and then puts it on top of his head to play the role of Abraham. He is constantly switching the wig/beard back and forth as he trades roles in his monologue.*)

GOD: I have a proposition for you Abraham.

ABRAHAM: Great! What's the plan?

GOD: I will make a Covenant with you and your people, and you will be the father of a great nation.

ABRAHAM: I like it. Is there more?

GOD: Yes. I will make you very fruitful and I will give unto you and your Descendents the whole of Canaan. It is a land flowing with milk and honey.

ABRAHAM: Uh, yes, but aren't the Canaanites already living there?

GOD: So kill them and drive them out of it.

ABRAHAM: But what about The Ten Commandments, you know, "Thou shalt not kill?"

GOD: I meant, "Thou shalt not kill anyone who worships me!" Everyone else is fair game.

ABRAHAM: Yes. I knew that. So when do we attack?

GOD: Tomorrow. I will help you in battle.

ABRAHAM: Great! I'll tell the men.

GOD: Of course, I will expect something in return.

ABRAHAM: Of course.

GOD: There are three things I will require of you. First, you and your people must obey all of The Commandments that I have given you.

ABRAHAM: Consider it done.

GOD: Second, you and your people must have no other gods before me.

ABRAHAM: Sounds fair enough…and the last thing?

GOD: Yes, I was getting to that.

ABRAHAM: Speak it and it shall be done. We live only to serve your Will.

GOD: I'm glad to hear you say that, because I need for you and your men to cut off the ends of your penises!

(*Big laughs from all the women in the audience. The men boo and hiss.*)

ABRAHAM: (*After a moment of stunned silence*) I might have to talk that one over with the guys.

(*More laughter from the audience.*)

ORLAN: (*Waits for the audience to settle*). Of course I'm only kidding. Man or woman, circumcision was probably one of God's better ideas if you think about it. As any good psychiatrist will tell you, the average male thinks about his penis at least once every fifteen minutes, and as an average male, I'll tell you it's the truth. So when God tells you to cut off a piece of your manhood so that it's going to be even shorter than it was before, that's something you're definitely going to remember. And that's the whole point. Now whenever a man thinks about his penis, he can't help but imagine how much larger it might have looked if part of it wasn't missing, and he can't help but remember that it was God who wanted it trimmed. But you women have to be careful out there. The next time some guy in a bar, or even in a church, tells you that he thinks about God every fifteen minutes, don't automatically assume that he's a priest!

(*Again, big laughs from all the women.*)

ORLAN: But then again, maybe God is a woman after all, and She just has penis envy!

(*More laughs from the men in the audience this time.*)

WARNING

It is important to remember that most of Orlan's fans are fairly well drunk by the time he begins his routine, so if you're reading this book sober and find Orlan's brand of irreverent comedy to be completely devoid of all humor, you might want to stop here and have a few beers and try reading it again. If you don't drink you might want to skip the rest of this chapter altogether. And if your blood-alcohol level is already above the legal limit for operating a motor vehicle and you still haven't managed even a modest chuckle by now, it might gratify you to know that you're not alone.

God didn't laugh at any of Orlan's jokes either.

As I said, God hates Orlan Fritz. And to make this point perfectly clear, He brings a curse down upon Orlan's head (and here's the part where the problem of Relative Simultaneity comes in). In Psalms: 10, David wonders why God stands so far off.

Perhaps it is to gain a better perspective of the world of men, but in so doing, He falls prey to the uncertainties of Relative Simultaneity. God is standing still, wherever He is, but the Earth is moving, or the Earth is moving at one speed and God is moving at another speed. His vision is skewed. He sees two lightning bolts flash instead of one. He hurls the curse, but His timing is off.

Instead of killing Orlan, the curse strikes a steel belted radial tire on a car that is passing in front of the bar where Orlan is performing his nightly comedy routine. The tire blows out, causing the car to skid out of control, smash into a lamppost, and overturn into a ditch. The driver of the car, miraculously, is still alive and manages to crawl out of the wreckage with only a few minor scrapes and bruises.

Once he is at a safe distance from the car, he tries to phone for help, but can't get a signal on his cell-phone, so he goes into the bar to see if he can find a payphone, when he overhears Orlan's comedy routine on stage.

The driver turns out to be Karlton Henderson, the famous Hollywood movie and television producer. Karlton is so amused by Orlan's act that he forgets about his car and stays after the show to offer Orlan a spot on the late night television talk show, *Night Owls with Ralph Barnhill.*

Orlan accepts the invitation and the network loves him. He becomes an overnight success story. Within a year's time he has his own top rated television sitcom, which is scheduled in the enviable Super-Sized-Super-

Sunday primetime lineup. Soon a multimillion-dollar book and movie deal is in the works. Orlan takes all of this good fortune as a sign that God has a terrific sense of humor and really enjoys his act.

God wants to set the record straight!

He blasts another curse at Orlan, but once again, Relative Simultaneity has twisted God's view of Earthly reality. Orlan's book, *Mr. Irreverence*, becomes a national sensation. It hits the top of the New York Times bestseller list. His sitcom wins an Emmy. Entertainment magazines are abuzz with rumors of an Academy Award in Orlan's future. God is beside himself with rage and frustration.

In the days of Abraham and Moses, Relative Simultaneity was not the problem that it is today, because in those days God was actually standing on the Earth when He worked his miracles and brought His wrath down upon the heads of His enemies. It was only about the time of King David, when God began standing far off, that complications due to Relative Simultaneity became noticeable.

There was another factor too. In those earlier times, God seemed more concerned with group sin rather than the sin of one individual person; God flooded all of the Earth to punish the wicked; He scattered all of mankind from the Tower of Babel to punish the arrogant; He brought down plagues against all of Egypt; He destroyed all of Sodom and Gomorrah; He sent all of Israel to wander in exile in the wilderness for forty years.

These kinds of punishments, though effective, require little accuracy to execute successfully. But when you're standing far off from the Earth and attempting to strike down just one man who is moving in a crowd of millions that is also moving, while trying to compensate for the uncertainties caused by Relative Simultaneity, that is a different matter altogether. The odds of hitting your mark are not so good!

The best way of ensuring success is to have someone who is standing on the Earth, someone whom you trust, to kill the transgressor for you; hence, the law in Leviticus directing the stoning of blasphemers. But God sees that no one on the Earth is going to be stoning Orlan dead any time soon (something about a misinterpretation of the, "Thou shalt not Kill" Commandment) and so God decides that it might be best to do the job Himself—before Orlan gets elected Pope!

Generally, God does not like going down to the Earth because He has found that being seen by men does little to inspire obedience, or even fear, and usually results only in the creation of more religions, which is the last thing mankind needs. Case in point, God's original plan was that there be only one religion on the planet, and the last time He counted He was certain the total came up to more than fifty.

There is another reason God doesn't like going down to Earth. The last time He visited, they nailed Him to a cross and stuck a spear in His side. Since then, taking physical form gives Him pounding headaches and severe nausea, but the situation with Orlan has gotten out of hand. Orlan has made it personal. The time has come to take matters into His own Hands.

Several angels offer to go in His place, but He refuses them all, saying to them in a thunderous voice, "Vengeance is mine, saith The Lord!"

"Mind your temper," they say to Him.

He neither looks back to them nor does He respond.

It is 11:00 P.M., Eastern Standard Time, and God is sitting in a 1962 Volkswagen Beetle that He has hot-wired and stolen from HONEST ABE'S USED CAR LOT (God knows that there is nothing honest about Honest Abe, which is why He took the car).

Fighting back the urge to vomit and suffering through one of the worst migraines He has ever had, God waits as Orlan Fritz steps out of a local shopping plaza with an armload of groceries in both hands. Orlan stops at the curb and God waves at him to cross at the stop sign. When he does, God guns the engine and knocks Orlan to the pavement, backing over him once for good measure.

There is a brief high-speed chase on the interstate before God steers the Beetle off an overpass and onto the street below where it explodes on impact and burns furiously. The smell of charred rubber and burning fuel rise skyward like smoke from a burnt offering. It is an aroma God finds pleasing to His nostrils and He smiles down from Heaven at the havoc He has just wreaked.

"Now that's comedy!" He says.

Bertram first recorded this story in a spiral notebook he entitled *God Stories* by Bertram Grey. He wrote down other things in it too; thoughts as they came to his mind; short fables that questioned all of The Old Answers to all of The Old Questions; weekly critiques of all of The Sunday Sermons that his Uncle Jacob had given; jokes that he found amusing; small poems intended as lyrics to songs for which he would one day write the music; and a criminal number of limericks with questionable ethical implications and even more questionable rhyming schemes.

By the end of his junior year in high school, Bertram had the pages of this notebook filled, and was starting on a second notebook when Jacob, while setting a mousetrap in the guestroom, found the first notebook behind a bookcase where Bertram had hidden it. And being a good parent, Jacob read it. He was justifiably horrified, but after careful consideration decided that it would be best to return the notebook to its place behind the bookcase and to put the mousetrap under the bed.

The next day Jacob invited Bertram to go fishing.

CHAPTER 6

Half a mile south of Temple Creek Baptist Church, Temple Creek widened to form a small lake, not quite large enough to earn a name of its own, but still large enough so that everyone referred to it as a lake instead of a pond. It was there, very early on Saturday morning, that Jacob took Bertram fishing.

They stood on the roots of a large oak that extended out into the water forming a natural pier. Casting and reeling their lines near the edge of a patch of brown reeds that formed an island at the center of the lake, they spoke quietly in the morning mists, so as not to disturb the serenity of the moment or the disposition of the fish. But the fish were not in a mood to be caught that day.

"I guess they decided to sleep in," Bertram said.

"Fish don't sleep in, Son," Jacob said.

"Not even on Saturday mornings?"

"Not even on holidays," Jacob said. "It's a scientific fact."

"Oh," Bertram said, not believing him.

"It's true. And what do you suppose restless fish think about all night long while they're swimming around in circles?"

"Calculus?"

"No. They think about breakfast—which is good for us—because by the time morning rolls around, they're so hungry from thinking about it that they'll swallow anything you dangle in front of them, sharp edges and all, which is why fishermen, like us, get up so early in the morning to catch them."

"And because fishermen, like us, want to get out of the house before they have to clean out the garage like Mother Liz wants them to?" Bertram said.

"Yes, that too," Jacob said, and he gave Bertram a conspiratorial wink as he cast his line out into the water again. "Genius is, after all, the hallmark of any good fisherman, and as any good fisherman will tell you, it's as important to know your wife as well as you know your fish."

"Yes, Father, I can see how that would be something useful to know."

Bertram had been watching a small flock of sparrows that had entered the clearing just above the surface of the lake. He watched them scattering and regrouping, settling here and there, forming and unforming intricate patterns of dance as they moved along the arc of the opposite shoreline.

The birds had settled just above the reed-island now, hovering over it like a restless cloud, and then perhaps, sensing that Bertram's attention had turned to them, the flock scattered again, regrouped, and veered off unexpectedly above the treetops.

Bertram had enjoyed witnessing this bit of chaotic beauty while it lasted, and for a moment as equally fleeting, and for a reason he didn't quite understand, he suddenly felt very happy. Such moments, he knew from past experiences, never lasted for very long, but he had learned to appreciate them when they came and not to pine for them when they passed, as they must always pass. So he stood there beside his uncle, enjoying the moment until it was lost to him, and when it was gone, he turned his mind to more pressing and sober thoughts.

For a time they fished together in silence, Jacob standing farther out on the root-pier of the oak and Bertram watching him with reverent admiration, recalling the happy moments they had spent together: Bertram calling him Father and Jacob calling him Son. It was a pleasant little dream even though Bertram knew that it wasn't really true, and he wondered, should he mourn its passing when reality finally came to wake him, as he knew it must one day, perhaps even this day? Would today be the day when the happy dream would finally come to an end?

Jacob said, "I noticed you haven't come by to ask me any questions lately. Has someone else been answering them for you?"

"No, I just sort of figure them out for myself these days."

"What were you thinking about just now?"

"Nothing important."

"I glanced over and saw your face. It didn't look like nothing."

Bertram shrugged. "It was just a thought."

"A question then?"

"No, not really."

"If something is troubling you, Son, you should tell me what it is. That's why I'm here, remember?"

"Yes, I remember."

"Then tell me."

As a child, Bertram did not like fairy tales with happy endings and make-believe games with imaginary people. These things were not real and he did not like being deceived by optimistic dreams that presented life in an unrealistic way.

If a thing was believed to be true and real, and the time came for it to be tested to see if it was as real as it was believed to be, then it must be tested, even if the test might destroy the thing, no matter how pleasant or how beautiful a thing it was. This did not bother Bertram, for he was well acquainted with the sting of disappointment and he had no fear of loss, for why should he feel regret over the loss of a thing that had not truly existed in the first place?

"Okay then," Bertram said. "I will tell you. I was thinking about what you said, about the fish. How they don't sleep in, even on holidays."

"And you thought it was funny?"

Bertram was smiling now. "No," he said, "I thought it was a lie."

"Oh," Jacob said. "I see." He smiled too.

"But it made me think of something else," Bertram said. "I thought about Jesus and The Disciples, that among all the people of the world, He chose fishermen, the most notorious of all liars, and appointed them with the task of proclaiming to all the world God's Truth. It's a wonder that anyone believed them at all."

Jacob said, "It was because they spoke the truth that they were believed, so you see, it's really no great surprise. People recognize the truth when they hear it, no matter who is telling it. Some may try to deny it, but they know in their hearts what is true and what is not, what is good and what is evil. Had The Disciples spoken lies, no one would have believed them. But they were believed, which only goes to prove that they were telling the truth."

"Or to prove that they were just very good liars. And maybe that's exactly what Jesus wanted; fast talking salesmen to sell his new idea about God to the Jews and eventually to the whole world."

"Is that what you believe, Bertram?"

"Sometimes I'm not so sure," Bertram said. "I ask myself, 'Was Jesus truly the Son of God or was he simply a man trying to change the world's flawed concept of God, from a God of Blood Sacrifice and War, to a God of Peace and Love, and in so doing, make the world a better place?' Since both views have the possibility of being true, without proof, how can you really be sure which one is real?"

"That's what faith is for," Jacob said. "Faith, like the ability to reason, is a gift from God. All men have it. But where reason gives us the ability to think, faith gives us the ability to overcome our doubts and to learn to trust in God for what we need. Both are gifts from God and both require practice so that they may be used effectively and with skill."

"Do you ever doubt, sometimes?"

"Yes, about some things."

"Like what?"

"There are times when I wonder if I'm being as faithful as I tell others to be. I like to believe I am, but then I wonder, 'If I am so faithful, then why can't my faith move mountains?'"

"I see," Bertram said. "You doubt yourself, not God."

"Of course. Who else should I doubt? God exists. Jesus is His son. God, through Christ, makes all things possible for those who believe in him. These are all facts, Bertram. So by the use of logic and reason, it must follow, that if my prayers remain unanswered, then the fault must lie within myself, doubt must lay within me somewhere, even if I am not aware of it."

"I understand," Bertram said, "and what do you do when you doubt?"

"I do what we all must do when we fall prey to sin, for doubting is a sin. I pray to Jesus for forgiveness and strength of faith, for Jesus is the only Path to Redemption."

"And what if that doesn't work?"

"Sometimes silence in itself is an answer, Bertram. God does not answer the prayers of prideful and arrogant people. You must ask yourself if you have committed a sin for which you have not yet repented," Jacob said. "Why? Is there something that you have been asking of God?"

"I've been asking for faith," Bertram said, too quickly, because as soon as he said the words, he realized his error. He should have said that he had been asking for "more faith" or for "stronger faith," but it was too late to take back the words now, and Bertram wondered if his uncle would catch the mistake.

"Has your prayer been answered?" Jacob said.

"No. It hasn't."

"Then you must reflect upon your past sins. You must ask yourself if there is something you may have said or done or maybe even *written* that may have been offensive to God, something for which you have not yet asked forgiveness," Jacob said. He looked into Bertram's eyes. "Is there anything you may have done that needs forgiving, Son?"

"No," Bertram said, without hesitation. "Nothing I can think of."

"Are you sure?"

Bertram thought very carefully before he answered the question a second time.

LETTERS TO SANTA AND DEADBEAT DADS

—A reading from The Gospel According to Bertram,
Book 1, Chapter 1—

When Bertram was very young, his mother (his real mother) taught him that there was a difference between magic and make-believe. Magic, true magic, was real. It was the result of unseen supernatural forces causing things to happen, like miracles and stigmata and visions from God. Angels and demons were supernatural beings. They were real. Ghosts and goblins were make-believe. They were not real.

She also taught him that The Tooth Fairy exchanged teeth for money, that The Easter Bunny brought him colored eggs and candy on Easter Morning, that Santa Claus brought him toys on Christmas Day, and that his father (his real father) would one day return to make things right and to be a family.

Now, Bertram had never seen God or Santa or Angels or The Easter Bunny, or even his own father, for that matter, but he still believed in them. Just because you couldn't see a thing, his mother had told him many times, didn't make it any less real, and he believed her because he trusted her and also because he had collected a substantial amount of circumstantial evidence over the years that seemed to support her testimony.

Most of his evidence came in the form of direct written correspondence with the supernatural beings that were most accessible to him. For example, besides his teeth, Bertram would leave small notes under his pillow with questions for The Tooth Fairy to answer. He did the same for The Easter Bunny and Santa Claus, asking similar questions to see if he could establish a pattern that might allow him a greater understanding into the workings of the unseen supernatural world.

His questions were varied, but always with a particular point in mind. Fairies had wings, but reindeer did not, yet each creature could fly. Was this because they used a different kind of magic or was it the same kind of magic only used in a different way? Bunnies had no thumbs, and yet The Easter Bunny could tie a bow expertly and without flaw. How was this possible? One theory: The fairies were helping him.

The big problem, Bertram found, with the supernatural world was that it seemed to make a distinct effort to remain mysterious and unexplainable. His questions, though always receiving a reply, were usually answered in the form of a riddle and were often times so vague as to be of little or no scientific value at all.

To his question concerning the magic of flying reindeer and fairies, the answer was, "A bumblebee and a hummingbird both can fly, but one has feathers and the other does not. On the matter of bunnies tying bows, it was, "A spider has no hands and yet it weaves tapestries of great beauty."

Bertram admitted that these kinds of answers did contain an element of truth, but they did little to help him acquire any real understanding of supernatural phenomenon. And seeing no other way to gather the information he needed, Bertram did as all good scientists who objectively seek the truth in accordance with the guidelines of The Scientific Method. He went on patiently collecting his evidences, filing them away for future study until the day he might, by some accident of discovery or sudden insight, uncover the critical key that would allow him to make some sense of them.

His contact with fairies abruptly came to an end when he ran out of baby teeth, and to make up for the loss he asked his mother to buy him a Ouija board so that he could talk to angels. But his mother became upset and told him that playing with Ouija boards was sinful and repugnant to God. He told her that he was sorry and at her direction prayed to God and to Jesus for forgiveness, though it did seem strange to him that wanting to talk to angels would be considered a sin.

Afterwards, he decided that it might be best to keep his future investigations into the supernatural world a secret from her. He did not want to worry her, and graver concerns looming before him meant that he would have to intensify his studies. With his connection to The Tooth Fairy gone, he began to see that the supernatural world was somehow linked to childhood, the bond growing weaker as people grew older.

His mother never received gifts from Santa or The Easter Bunny, only he did. Because he was a child and she was not. How much longer, he wondered, before he lost contact with them as well? Time was a factor. That was obvious now. If he was to find an answer it would have to be through what clues he could gather from Santa and The Easter Bunny while they still remained accessible to him.

One Christmas morning, while adding his most recent acquisition to his Santa File—a Q-tip that he had swabbed around the rim of a mug of cold cocoa from which Santa had allegedly drank—he considered what part time job might be available to him after school so that he could earn enough money to send it off to a laboratory to have it tested, when suddenly, he realized that he had been approaching his investigations of the supernatural world from entirely the wrong end.

The reason he had been getting no meaningful answers to his questions all these years was that he had been asking the wrong "people." He should have been presenting his questions directly to God, since it was God who had created the natural and the supernatural worlds. Bertram wasted no time in correcting his error. He set to work that morning composing his next letter, this one, to God Himself.

Using his mother's best stationery and testing six ink pens before finding one that had just the right color and sharpness of line, Bertram began his letter with a formal apology, in the event that God may have been offended by his shortsighted attempt to find his own answers rather than first consulting Him with his questions.

Next, to avoid the risk of snubbing God a second time, Bertram made a number of positive comments on world events, and on a more personal level, complimented God on some of His more obscure and largely uncelebrated works; those small details in everyday life that everyone enjoys, and yet too few bother to even acknowledge, much less give thanks for having; like the taste of raspberries and bananas when you eat them together, and the warm smell of green grass baking in the heat of a summer afternoon, little things Bertram knew that God had taken great care in creating, yet for which He had received little or no recognition.

From there, Bertram ended the letter on a quick note (so as not to appear to be dwelling too much on his own needs) by submitting an itemized list of all of the questions he had ever had regarding the supernatural world. He signed it:

Humbly Awaiting Your Reply,

With a Sincere and Honest Heart,
I am Very Truly Yours,

Bertram Gray

When he was done, he reviewed the letter with great care, and being satisfied with his work, meticulously blew on each page until he was sure the ink was dry so it would not smear when he folded the letter and placed it inside the envelope. Then using a minimal amount of saliva so that the edge of the flap would have a smooth, clean appearance, he sealed it and turned it over and wrote GOD in big block letters on the front side of the envelope.

He used HEAVEN as the address and didn't bother with a zip code, feeling that it was unnecessary, owing to the fact that there was only one God and only one Heaven. He did put an extra stamp on it, thinking that the added postage might help to get it there more directly. He would have liked to have asked his mother for some advice on the matter, but remembered how severely she had reacted when he first tried communicating with angels, and not wanting to upset her needlessly, he waited for her to go to work and mailed the letter in secret. He waited three months for a reply.

But God never answered him.

After six months had passed, curiosity finally got the best of him and he decided to tell his mother what he had done in the hope that she might know why God had never answered his letter. When he told her, he was very happy to see that she was not upset by what he had done, and even happier when she told him that, "Yes, indeed," she did know exactly the answer to his question.

She told him that God answered letters in a different way than Santa or The Tooth Fairy or The Easter Bunny did. God didn't use paper to answer a letter. To God, writing a letter was just like saying a prayer and so He answered both in the same way. This explanation made a lot of sense to Bertram because it did seem to be in agreement with what he knew of God from what he had read in his Bible, heard in Church, and seen in the movies.

From his Sunday school lessons, Bertram knew that his mother was right when she told him that God did not use paper to write letters. He used stone. He wrote The Ten Commandments in stone. And having seen the movie version of The Ten Commandments and witnessing God's fiery penmanship on film, Bertram understood quite well why stone was necessary (plain paper simply would have not withstood the process).

But stone or paper, the fact remained that God could write letters when He wanted to. So Bertram consoled himself with the idea that if God had written him a letter, the post office would have probably never been able to deliver it to him anyway, since stone tablets that size would have never fit in his mailbox.

By the time Bertram was nine, he had attended five different elementary schools because his mother and he moved around a lot, but no matter where they went, it never ceased to amaze Bertram how Santa Claus and The Easter

Bunny were always able to find them. His mother told him that it was because Santa had a magic telescope and The Easter Bunny had a magic crystal egg that allowed them to see anyone anywhere in the world no matter where they had moved.

The children at the schools, however, told Bertram that the real reason that Santa and The Easter Bunny were always able to find him was because there was no Santa Claus and there was no Easter Bunny. It was his mother pretending they were real, just for fun. Bertram didn't believe them at first, but the seed of doubt had been planted in his mind and he began to see the world in a different way.

Things began to make more sense to him. For example, it explained why people used science to build automobiles and airplanes to travel from one place to another instead of using the magic of flying reindeer and blue fairies. It explained why candy stores and toy stores seemed to be more crowded in March and December than any other time of the year. And Bertram wondered, "Was this the great secret concerning the mystery of The Supernatural; the critical key that would finally make sense of it all? That it never really existed? That it was all just make-believe and pretend?"

But if this were the case, then it meant that his mother, whom he trusted and loved, had lied to him, and the children at school, whom he didn't much care for, were telling him the truth. This wasn't entirely inconceivable to Bertram, because he knew that sometimes the people who loved you, lied to you to make you happy, and the people who hated you, told you the truth to make you sad.

But who was telling the truth? Bertram had to know.

It was time, he decided, to reopen his files and resume his investigations. How would they appear, he wondered, with the magic stripped away from them? What would he see now that he had opened his mind to the possibility that his evidence might be nothing more than nursery fables and lies?

This did not mean that Bertram believed that his mother was lying to him, only that it was a possibility, and just because it was a possibility, did not make it true. Emotion had no place in science and Bertram knew that allowing cynicism to taint his perspective was no better than allowing hope or faith to contaminate his objectivity. Creating an answer to fit the question was not the same as finding the truth. Truth could not be forced. It must rise from the facts of its own volition and its authenticity must be so evident as to defy reproach.

To this end, Bertram did something that he had not done during his original study of the supernatural. He took his files: The Santa File, The Tooth Fairy File, and The Easter Bunny File, and he opened them up and spread them out on the floor of his bedroom so that he could see everything all at once, studying them as if they were one large continuous file, instead of three separate ones.

He stood over them, watching them, allowing his mind to take in the information, not searching for anything in particular, not thinking to find an answer, not hoping, not wanting, not forcing. He was merely looking, only observing what lay before him, waiting to see if some kind of pattern might emerge from the clutter and present itself to his unbiased, uncritical eye.

To his surprise, a pattern did emerge, almost immediately.

It was a simple pattern. A pattern so obvious and so visible that he was amazed that he had not noticed it before, but there it was, as it had always been, only he had not recognized it as an answer...until now.

He saw that Santa and The Tooth Fairy and The Easter Bunny all had the very same handwriting. A suspicion formed in his mind and he went into the kitchen to get his mother's grocery list. He took it from the yellow smiley face magnet that held it to the refrigerator door and he brought it to his bedroom. He laid it on the floor beside the rest of his evidence. And when he compared it, he saw that the handwriting on the list also matched the handwriting in each of his files.

But Bertram was not through. His mind was still hot with inspiration and he went into his closet to get the shoebox where he kept all of the things that his father had ever sent to him in the mail: letters and postcards, birthday cards and get well cards, and cards for every other important occasion in his life. Bertram opened up each letter and each card and he laid them beside his files one by one. And when he compared them to his mother's grocery list, as he had done with all of his other files, he wasn't very much surprised to find that the handwriting on all of his father's letters also matched the handwriting on the list.

And so it was on this day that Bertram discovered that Santa Claus, The Tooth Fairy, The Easter Bunny, and even his own father never really existed. They were all just fantasy creatures of a make-believe world that his mother had created to make him happy.

Bertram would have stopped believing in God on this day as well, but he reminded himself that there were still millions of other people in the world besides his mother who seemed to believe in Him too, which did lend some credibility to the idea. And there was one other thing that God had going for Him that the other creatures did not.

God had never written Bertram a letter.

FISHING FOR JESUS

Standing close to Bertram, looking into his face, Jacob realized how much his young nephew had grown. He was no longer the somber faced little boy, full of questions that he had found on his front porch swing that summer in July, five years earlier. He was a senior in high school now, possessing the intellect and the determination to fulfill his ambition of going to college after graduation. He was becoming a man, forming his own opinions about the world and acting on them with confidence. One day—a day when they would no longer stand together—Jacob knew that Bertram would have to make the choice that all men must make.

Jacob hoped that Bertram would make the right choice.

Jacob never doubted that Bertram would grow up to be a good man, of course, but then Hell was filled with the souls of good men with good intentions to make a better world. Good works alone did not save a man's soul. This was a point that Jacob had often tried to impress upon Bertram's young mind, and with their time together growing short, Jacob needed to know that Bertram understood this fact and believed it.

"You haven't given me an answer yet," Jacob said. "Did you think of something that needs forgiving?"

"No," Bertram said. "I was thinking that I do have a question for you, after all."

"What is it?"

"You said that God brought us together so you could answer my questions so that I may know Him better."

"Yes."

"So how do you know the answers? Where do you find them?"

"God speaks to me. He tells me the answers—not in the way He spoke with Moses, of course. I don't hear Voices or see Burning Bushes that tell me they are God. And even if I did and I told you about it, I'm sure you'd probably think I was crazy."

"Then how does He speak to you?"

"God has many voices, some of them we hear with our ears, some of them we see, and others we simply feel inside."

"I see," Bertram said, unaware that a smile had crept into the corners of his mouth.

"Did my answer amuse you?" Jacob said.

"No, it just reminded me of something that my mother told me once. It was about hummingbirds and bumblebees."

"What about them?"

"She was trying to explain something to me about things I couldn't see, like you are now. Only she didn't really explain anything. What she said sounded nice. Like a fairy tale with a happy ending. It's something that you'd like to believe is true, but no one really knows for sure."

"What are you trying to say, Son?"

"It's just that if you can't see God's lips moving when He's talking to you, then how can you really be sure that it's God who's doing the talking? It might be Satan trying to deceive you or your own mind playing tricks on you."

"Yes Bertram, that is true, to the unbelieving mind. But we, as believers, know the truth. We can tell the difference between what is of God and what is of man. It's just as The Apostle Paul once said, 'The mature, who because of practice, have their senses trained to discern good and evil.' You see, it is by continually striving for The Wisdom of God that we learn to see His image and to hear His voice in the things that seem only commonplace to the unbeliever. Tell me, Bertram, what is it that you see and hear?"

"I try to see and hear things as they are, not as I'd like them to be," Bertram said. "It seems to me that if faith alone can lead us to the truth, then it should lead us all to the same truth, but it doesn't. Even those people who call themselves Christian can't seem to agree on one version of the truth either, yet they all claim to know, without the slightest doubt, that their version of Christianity is more true than any of the others."

"Yes, that is very true."

"I think the problem is that the things that they think they know, they know only by faith, and by faith alone."

"No, that's not the problem, Bertram. The problem is that they place their faith in the wrong things. Yes, they know what they know by faith, and by faith alone, but it's a misguided faith. Faith, Bertram, is a power, and like any power, it can be corrupted. Their faith is corrupt because they have chosen to place it in the wrong things."

"I'm sure they'd probably say the same thing about you, if I asked them."

"I'm sure they would too, but that doesn't make them right."

"But how can you know that?"

"Bertram," Jacob said, gently.

"Yes, Father?"

"I once asked you if you had been saved and you told me that you were, but you don't sound like someone who has been saved."

Bertram said, "When I was a baby, my mother had me baptized. She told me I was saved and I believed her, so I thought I was."

"And what do you think now?"

"I'm older now, and now I'm not so sure."

Jacob laid a hand on Bertram's shoulder. He said, "Being saved is a choice, Son. It's a choice that no one else can make for you. You have to make it for yourself."

"Then I'm not saved?"

"No, Son. You're not."

"Yes," Bertram said. "I think you must be right, because I don't feel saved."

"Do you want to be saved?"

"I'm not sure if I even know what that means anymore—being saved—but I know what I *do* want."

"What is that?"

"I want to be able to look up at the sky and *know* that there really is Someone out there, looking down at me from Heaven or Wherever, watching out for me. I want to *know* that there is something beyond death and that it's better than this life, but then I guess that's what everyone wants, really. They're afraid of dying, afraid of being alone, and so they pretend that there's something more. It makes them feel better, so they believe it. I'd like to believe it too. It'd be nice to know those things, you know, but..."

"But you can believe it, Son. If you want to."

"How?"

"You have to *want* to believe it."

"I do want to believe it."

"Then you're almost there. Now all you have to do is to give yourself completely to God. Stop trying to figure out things that you were never meant to know. It only vexes your spirit. Remember, it is by faith alone that we are saved, not by knowledge."

"So what do I do, just stop thinking?"

"No. Stop doubting. Stop questioning every little detail. Let God take care of the universe. Just live your life as Jesus has instructed you to live it. That's all the knowledge that God expects you to have. Nothing else matters. For once, put your fate entirely into God's hands. Take that leap of faith. I assure you. He will be there to catch you when you do."

"Are you sure?" Bertram said.

"Yes, I am. God wants you to believe in Him. He wants you to be saved, but you have to be willing to let Him come into your heart."

"I do. I do want Him to come into my heart."

"Then follow me into the water and let me baptize you in Jesus' name. Choose for yourself now to become saved and you will see that what I am telling you is true."

"Okay," Bertram said, and not permitting himself to spoil the moment by pursuing a second thought, he took Jacob's hand without question and waded out into the lake with him. When they were waist deep in water, they stopped and faced each other and Jacob said, "Are you ready, Son?"

"Yes. I am," Bertram said.

Jacob stepped around Bertram and took him in his arms, supporting him in baptismal fashion. Bertram closed his eyes and held his nose and took a short breath and readied himself to receive the blessings of faith, but just as Jacob was about to baptize Bertram, Jacob made the mistake of asking Bertram a question.

Jacob said, "Bertram, do you accept Jesus Christ as your Personal Savior and do believe that He is the Son of God sent down from Heaven to die for your sins so that you may have eternal life?"

And Bertram, being the honest person that he was, had no choice but to answer the question truthfully. He said, "No. No, I don't believe it, but I want to."

This was not exactly the answer that Jacob had been expecting to hear, and he froze where he was, with Bertram in his arms just inches above the surface of the water. Bertram, sensing that something had gone awry, opened his eyes and looked up at his uncle, and said, "Is something wrong, Father?"

"I thought you said you wanted to be saved," Jacob said.

"I do."

"Then why did you say you didn't believe?"

"Because I don't believe. I told you that. Remember? I said that I didn't believe, but that I wanted to. That's why I want to be saved. So that I will believe."

"But you have to believe first before I can baptize you."

"Why is that?"

"Because that's what God expects of us, Bertram." Jacob withdrew his arm from around Bertram's shoulder and let him stand on his own. Jacob said, "First you choose to believe and then you get baptized. That's the way it works. Those are God's rules. You can't go on making up your own rules and then expect God to honor them. Besides, why would you want to make a commitment to God, if you don't even believe that He exists?"

"So that God will see that I'm trying to believe in Him. I thought it might help."

"God gives every man a measure of faith."

"I know, but…"

"Well, it's true, Son."

"Then why can't I believe?"

"Only God can answer that question, Son. Why don't we ask Him?" Jacob said, and he reached out to Bertram and took his hands and together they bowed their heads and they prayed very earnestly for almost ten minutes, while the sleepless fish in the lake, circled them curiously looking for something to eat.

When they had finished praying, Jacob said, "Did you find any answers?" Bertram thought for a moment, searching his mind for something that hadn't been there before, but everything seemed the same. "No," he said. "I didn't."

"I think I know the reason that God has not answered your prayer, Bertram."

"You do?"

"Yes. I found the book you had hidden in your room behind the bookcase," Jacob said. "I was setting a mousetrap when I found it by accident."

"I know," Bertram said. "I always put it back a certain way. I could tell someone had moved it. I wasn't sure if it was you or Mother."

"I read it," Jacob said.

"Did you show it to Mother?"

"No."

"Will you?"

"Do you want me to?"

"No. I don't want to worry her."

"Then I won't."

"Thank you," Bertram said. "Sometimes it's best not to know things, only to believe in them."

"It's always best to know the truth, Bertram. The problem is, is that not everyone is always ready to hear it."

"I'm ready to hear it," Bertram said. "But first I need to know that it's real before I can believe it."

"God is real and I can prove it to you, Bertram."

"How?"

"Come home with me. Together we will burn that terrible thing that you have written against God. Then we will pray again and ask Him to forgive you. You have to repent for your sin, Bertram. Only then will God allow Jesus to come into your heart so that you can believe."

"He never came into my heart before I wrote it. Why should burning it now make any difference?"

"Because those things were in your heart before you wrote them on paper, only then, they were hidden. You are right; burning it alone will change nothing. You must also burn it out of your heart as well. You must confess your sin before men and before God and ask God to forgive you.

"You must give up your pursuit of these destructive thoughts, for they only hinder your relationship with God and unknowingly deliver you into the hands of Satan. Are you willing to do that, Bertram? To turn away from your old life and your old way of thinking and ask God to forgive you? Are you willing to humble yourself before God and before men, and give your mind, body, and soul completely to The Lord?"

"Yes," Bertram said. "But I'm not so sure God will listen."

"Why do you say that?"

"Doesn't the Bible say that when we ask something of God, that we must ask, 'in faith, nothing wavering, for the man who doubts is like a wave blown on the sea, and that man should not expect to receive anything from The Lord?'"

"Yes, the book of James does say that."

"So how can I can ask in faith, 'nothing wavering,' when it is faith that I am asking for? If James is right about God, then my prayer for faith will never be answered unless I can ask for it without doubting. But if I could do that, then I wouldn't need to ask for it in the first place. It seems to me like God is playing games. It's like He's forcing me to run a race that I can never win."

"No. That's not true, Son. There is a way."

"How?"

"I will pray for you."

"Will that work?"

"Yes, it will."

"How do you know?"

"Why would God create a means for men to redeem their souls and then deny them the ability to make use of it?"

"I don't know. Why would He do that?"

"Don't you see, Son? The answer is: He wouldn't do it. You're searching for the answer to a question that is in itself absurd. It's like asking, 'Why is the moon made of green cheese?' The answer is: It isn't. God wants you to believe in Him. He has given you the ability to do so, but He allows you to make the final choice. 'Seek and you will find; Ask and it shall be given.' That is the true answer to your question."

Bertram thought about this answer.

Jacob said, "You say you need to know that God is real before you can believe in Him. Well, that is what I'm offering to you now, a way of *testing* that what I'm telling you is true. Isn't that what you asked for?"

"Yes."

"Then come home with me today, this very moment, so that we may do what must be done. The eternal life that God wants you to have is in peril. To wait another day may cause you to lose it forever. 'No man can know the hour or the day,' The Scriptures say. Tomorrow may be too late."

"Yes," Bertram said. "I know."

"Then you'll come?"

"No, not just yet. I'd like to stay here a while longer, alone. I need some time to...pray...and to think...about what you've said."

"Don't stay too long, Son. Your Mother will worry."

Bertram smiled awkwardly. "I won't, Father. I'll be home soon. I promise."

"I know you will, Son. And I know you will make the right choice. I'll be waiting for you when you do."

Bertram smiled again and watched Jacob turn away reluctantly and go. He listened to the crush, crush, crush, of his uncle's footsteps until they could be heard no more. Then slowly, Bertram slipped back into the cold water and waded out from beneath the shade of the oak to a place where he could look up and see the sky.

Surely his uncle had been mistaken about God, Bertram thought, as he watched the clouds moving high above him. He was, after all, supposed to be a loving God. That's what people said about Him. Wouldn't God want him to be honest about how he felt and about what he believed? Bertram wondered which was worse, to be a lying believer, or a truthful unbeliever?

Neither option seemed good.

And Bertram truly did want to believe, but he felt that it was important to let God know that he was trying, despite what his uncle had told him. So to demonstrate the sincerity of his intentions, if not before men, at least before himself and before God (if He truly was up there), Bertram looked up to the sky and said, "I want to believe in you."

Then he closed his eyes, and he held his nose, and he took a short breath, and he baptized himself in the name of The Father and of The Son and of The Holy Spirit.

CHAPTER 7

Bertram's writings had been completely misunderstood by his Uncle Jacob. Bertram was not trying to be arrogant or disrespectful towards God. He was not trying to mock God in any way. He was simply trying to present the God of The Old Testament in a Twentieth Century setting to show how the understanding of God as set forth in The Old Testament was flawed.

Of course God would never steal a car and use it to run down a man who was telling bad jokes about Him. That was the whole point of the story, to demonstrate this flawed understanding of God.

It was the same message that Jesus had tried to tell the people of his time, that God was not a cruel and vengeful God, but a loving and compassionate God. The only difference was that Jesus never used humor as a means of delivering his message. And, judging by the reaction that Bertram had received from his uncle, Bertram could see why Jesus intentionally and completely avoided humor as a means of conveying it. Humor was so often misunderstood that the message could become lost in the telling of it.

And if Jacob had misunderstood Bertram's telling of it, then perhaps that was the reason that Bertram had gained no measurable amount of faith since baptizing himself in the lake, two weeks earlier. Maybe God had also misunderstood his message and was waiting for Bertram to atone for his sin (as his Uncle Jacob had suggested) before allowing Bertram to receive the gift of faith.

This was a very real possibility, and Bertram had to take it in earnest. Truth in The Name of Science demanded it! Though secretly, Bertram hoped that his uncle was wrong about God, and that God had a more developed sense of humor. But hope was not truth and Bertram knew that the only way to find out if his uncle was right or wrong about God was to do as his uncle had said, and to test it.

At first it seemed to Bertram that this kind of test might be considered a sin as well, because it was born of doubt. But then he remembered that even Gideon tested God, and not just once, but three times, and that The Apostle Paul himself once told the Thessalonians that they should, "Test everything," and, "Hold on to the good," which was exactly what Bertram intended to do. He would test everything.

CHRISTIAN SCIENCE AND THE SCIENTIFIC METHODIST

Bertram decided to begin his test on a Tuesday morning. He chose Tuesday morning because he knew that his Aunt Elizabeth would be away, as she usually was on most Tuesdays, visiting Pietyville Memorial Hospital and Christian Refuge for the Aged to witness to the community's sick and elderly residents. She was still unaware of Bertram's fallen state and he wished to keep it that way so as not to worry her.

Bertram had considered waiting until the following Saturday when he knew she would also be away, attending her monthly meeting with the church's garden club. But Jacob's warning that "No man can know the hour or the day," and that, "Tomorrow may be too late," weighed heavily upon Bertram's mind, and so quite reasonably, he was anxious to get started.

Matters were slightly complicated when Tuesday finally did arrive, bringing with it the season's first frost. But Bertram was ready for it, having watched the weather report on the evening news the previous afternoon, and he was up an hour earlier than usual to assist his aunt just in case she had trouble starting the car or needed help scraping ice from the windows. Everything went smoothly and Bertram saw to it that she was out of the house on schedule without any great fuss.

He smiled and waved to her from the front porch swing as she backed out of the driveway and, after she was gone, waited a few minutes more before proceeding with his plan, in the event that she may have forgotten something and decided to return home unexpectedly. When all seemed safe, he went back into the house and got what he needed from his room and crept down the hallway to look in on his uncle who was in the den, seated in the chair by the fireplace. He was drinking a cup of coffee and reading the morning paper.

"Hello Father," Bertram said.

Jacob looked up from his paper and smiled at Bertram. "Hello Son," he said. "Shouldn't you be getting ready for school?"

"I am ready."

"Got up a little earlier than usual today? That's good."

"Yes, I was helping Mother with the car. You should see the frost outside. It's so thick, it almost looks like snow." Bertram shivered a little, but not from the cold. "Maybe we could start a fire," he said, "you know, to take the chill out of the house."

"No need. You'll be gone soon and I like these brisk mornings. The cold stimulates my thoughts," Jacob said. "Besides, I doubt you'd have the time. The bus should be here any minute now. It's almost seven-thirty."

"It's seven fifteen. There's still time. It won't take long."

"There isn't any wood in the fireplace."

"I know. I meant to feed the fire with these," Bertram said and he removed two spiral notebooks from the inside of his coat pocket and set them on his uncle's lap. "I'm ready to burn them now."

Jacob picked up the notebooks and leafed through them. "There are two of them?"

"Yes. I'd filled one and was starting another. I had it with me when you found the first one. That's why you didn't see it."

"Oh," Jacob said.

"I was waiting for Mother to leave. I thought now might be a good time to do it."

"Do you want me to help you?"

"No, I think it might be best if I do it myself."

"Yes. I think so too."

Jacob returned the notebooks to Bertram and Bertram tucked them under his arm and knelt on the hearth to move the brass screen out of the way. He opened the first notebook and carefully placed it inside of the fireplace with the pages facing up. "Would you like me to hand you a match?" Jacob said.

"Yes. Thank you."

Jacob took a long wooden kindling match from the mantel and handed it to Bertram and Bertram struck it on the hearth. He lit pages on both sides, watching in silence as the paper shriveled and twisted in the flames, first one layer then the next.

"You understand, Bertram," Jacob said, "that burning these books will make no difference to God unless you learn to change what's in your heart."

"Yes, I know. But I have to start somewhere."

"That is true," Jacob said.

When the fire slowed and the flames began to stagnate, Bertram took a poker from the stand. He lifted the pages so they would burn more efficiently, prodding here and there from time to time to help the fire do its work, until nothing was left but curled pieces of broken ash and a spirally wound blackened wire.

Bertram struck another match and repeated the process with the second book, adjusting the flames as necessary with the poker, watching the notebook burn with no more regret or hesitation in his movements than he would have had, had he been burning a piece of kindling. When the job was done he placed the poker in its stand and moved the brass screen back in front of the fireplace.

"There," he said. "It's finished."

"How do you feel, Son?"

"The same," Bertram said, "but then, that was the easy part."

"Yes. In some ways I suppose it was, but the first step is important too. It determines your direction. You have decided to follow a path that leads to God."

"I have always sought a Path to God."

"I know, but now you understand that there is only One True Path. Sometimes we must travel down other roads and see for ourselves that they lead nowhere before we can believe what is true and follow it."

"Yes, I guess I've always been that way, you know, a kind of doubting Thomas. I have to go there and see it for myself before I can believe it."

"Blessed are the poor in spirit," Jacob said, "for theirs is The Kingdom of Heaven."

"Blessed are the pure in heart," Bertram said, "for they shall *see* God."

"Yes, that is also true. Faith and sincerity of heart go hand in hand, Bertram. God expects us to have both."

Bertram looked away.

"Is something wrong?"

"No, I think I hear the bus coming," Bertram said and he left the den to go check. Moments later he was back, standing in the doorway. "It's here. I've got to go now." The bus driver sounded the horn three times.

"We'll talk again later," Jacob said, "when you get home tonight."

"Yes," Bertram said. "When I get home." He paused in the doorway as if to say something more, smiled briefly, and was gone again. In the living room, he collected his schoolwork from the coffee table in front of the sofa, made a quick detour through the dining room to grab his lunch from the kitchen table, and ran outside to catch the bus.

RESULTS OF THE TEST

Faith never did come to Bertram, though he had done exactly as his uncle had instructed him. He burned the stories he had written, he worked to change his way of thinking and he prayed to God to change his heart so that he would no longer have the questions that constantly plagued his mind, but the questions never did go away. Still, he fought them, as he had promised he would do.

Now, whenever a disruptive thought entered his mind, he no longer dwelled upon it, but dismissed it immediately and recited The Lord's Prayer to himself. This technique worked very well, but it left Bertram feeling somewhat depressed every time he did it. And since prayer was supposed to uplift the soul and inspire feelings of hope, Bertram thought perhaps that he might be doing it wrong, so he went to his Uncle Jacob to see what might be the problem.

"What do you think might be the problem?" Jacob said.

"I don't know. Maybe it's because I don't really know what faith is."

"What do you think faith is?"

"I think that faith is the ability to believe in something, even when there's no proof to show that what you believe is true."

"No," Jacob said. "Faith is the assurance of things hoped for, the conviction of things not seen."

"Isn't that the same thing?"

"No," Jacob said. "It isn't Bertram. You say that you want to have faith, but then you say that you can't, because you can't believe in things that you can't see."

"Yes."

"But you believe in George Washington, don't you? And you never saw him."

"Yes."

"And to my knowledge, you've never been to the North Pole, but I suspect that you believe in that too?"

"Yes."

"Why? What's the reason?"

Bertram smiled, intrigued by his uncle's insight. "I don't know," he said. "That's a very good question. You're right, I *do* believe in them. Or do I? Maybe I just believe in the possibility of them?"

"Come on, Son. Either you believe in them or you don't. Which is it?"

"Okay. I guess I do believe in them, but I'm not so sure if faith is the reason."

"What other reason could it be? Faith is the conviction of things not seen. You have a conviction that George Washington once lived as a man and was the first President of The United States even though you weren't alive to see him firsthand. And you have a conviction that the North Pole is a real place that actually exists, even though you've never been there to see it either."

"Yes."

"And what do you base these convictions on?" Jacob said. "You base them solely on the assurance of other people who believe in them too. If that's not faith, then what is it?"

Bertram smiled again. "I don't know. Like I said, 'It's a good question.'"

"Think about it, Son," Jacob said. "Pray on it. I think you'll see I'm right."

Bertram said, "I will."

QUESTIONING THE QUESTION

The problem that Bertram had with faith was that he didn't know if it truly was a gift from God, as his uncle assured him it was, or whether it was merely a kind of protective reflex set up by the mind to help it cope with the ever present prospect of its own mortality; a gentle delusion caused by chemical reactions in the brain to trick itself into believing that death was as precious as life, and as meaningful.

For Bertram this was a critical distinction that had to be resolved before he could ever begin to believe in God, because unless he could first have faith in faith itself, he knew that he could never have faith in anything else.

But how to study such a thing as faith, a thing that could not be seen? Bertram knew that scientists often created machines to help them better understand the nature of things that could not be seen with the naked eye. They used incubators and electron microscopes to help them isolate and observe the mechanisms of disease causing viruses. They used particle accelerators and cloud chambers to allow them to view the internal workings of the atom.

What Bertram needed was a different kind of machine, one that could assist him in the discovery of the internal mechanisms of faith. He needed a device that could somehow allow him to capture faith in a test tube or to grow it artificially in a Petri dish so that he could examine it and test it and distill it from its religious impurities to see it for what it really was.

But faith was not a virus or a bacteria. (At least, for the moment, Bertram didn't believe that it was.) Faith was an idea, and as such, could be cultured and grown in only one kind of medium, the human brain. Though this restriction did seriously limit the means by which Bertram could approach the problem, it in no way rendered his project an impossibility, and in two weeks time he had all the details worked out on paper.

It took another two weeks to actually build the machine, a few days more to modify technical flaws in his original design and to finish the final adjustments. He asked his Uncle Jacob if he would be interested in volunteering for the position of lab rat for the machine's first operational test, since it had been his question that had inspired Bertram to build it. Jacob said that he'd be honored, providing he could have his brain back when Bertram was done with it.

Bertram said that he could.

THE FAITH MACHINE

The machine consisted of a six-by-six inch wooden vertical post, four feet high, which stood at the center of a plywood base, two feet by two feet square. Attached to one side of the post, near the top, was a Black Box with a lid and a trapdoor, and below it, directly underneath it, at the base of the post was a galvanized tin bucket, draped with blue Christmas tree lights. The bucket was tagged. The tag, a white label with black lettering, read: GRAVOMETER.

Next to the bucket, on the other side of the post was a twelve-volt car battery, from which, ran a series of switches and buttons connected together by white electrical wiring and black electrical tape. The switches were tagged in the same manner as the bucket, with black lettered names on white labels.

The labels read: ON/OFF SWITCH, START BUTTON, and TEST SWITCH.

Of particular interest, was the TEST SWITCH, for unlike any of the other switches, it was not electrically connected to the battery by any wiring. It hung completely isolated from the battery and the rest of the machine by a string tied to a picture hook that was attached to the wooden post just above the battery.

The final component of the machine was a magnetic ring that Bertram would wear on the middle finger of his right hand during the course of the experiment. The ring, a plain looking band with no decorative markings and a smooth flat space where a stone might have gone, had only one notable feature: Its color, a bright enamel red. It was painted red so that Jacob would clearly see it and be drawn into asking questions about it, questions that Bertram would leave largely unexplained so as to allow Jacob to find his own answers and in the process either prove or disprove Bertram's Hypothesis.

BERTRAM'S HYPOTHESIS AND THE PRINCIPLE OF AMORAL DECEIT

It was Bertram's Hypothesis that it was mystery, and not the Grace of God, that was responsible for inspiring faith. Without mystery, faith could not exist. This was the purpose of Bertram's faith machine, to provide a means of creating that mystery and at the conclusion of the experiment, confront Jacob with the choice of choosing either faith or reason as a means of resolving it.

Bertram hoped to lead Jacob into making this choice by walking him through a series of carefully staged predictions by using three items that were inside of the bucket; a shiny black stone, a plastic croquet ball, and a blue Ping-Pong ball. The predictions were designed to test Jacob's faith in The Law of Gravity.

In the final prediction, which would ultimately give Bertram the answer to the question that he sought, Bertram would use the blue Ping-Pong ball as the item to be tested in the Black Box. But in this prediction, the last prediction, there would be one critical, though seemingly minor, difference in the prediction process. Instead of using his left hand to place the Ping-Pong ball into the Black Box, as he would in all of the previous predictions, in this last prediction, Bertram would use his right hand, the hand on which he would wear the red enamel ring.

This was important because within the Ping-Pong ball, Bertram had inserted thin iron plates, which would allow The Ping-Pong ball to be picked up by a magnet. The ring that Bertram would wear during the course of the experiment contained a small magnet hidden inside of it, strong enough to pick up the Ping-Pong ball as Bertram removed his hand from the Black Box.

Bertram's hand would appear empty as he withdrew it from the box, giving the illusion that Bertram had placed the ball into the box, so when Bertram asked Jacob to predict whether the ball would stay in the box or fall into the bucket when the trapdoor was opened, any prediction that Jacob could make would be wrong.

This was one of the questions for which Bertram sought an answer: Would Jacob rely on his faith in God alone to make his final prediction, or would he admit the limits of his understanding, and choose to make a more reasonable choice: that is, to abandon his faith in God and admit to Bertram that without more knowledge, he could not reliably predict anything concerning the movement of the Ping-Pong ball, once the latch was flipped and the trapdoor opened.

But if Jacob choose to disregard reason, as Bertram suspected he would, any prediction that Jacob could make regarding the Ping-Pong ball would be proven to be wrong. And if faith could not be trusted to reveal the truth about something as insignificant as the location of a Ping-Pong ball, then how could it be trusted to reveal the truth about something as important as the existence of God? This was the ultimate question that Bertram really wanted answered as a result of his test.

How could his uncle still continue to believe in God by faith, when confronted with the fact that faith was fallible? It was a question that only a man of faith could answer for Bertram. And because Bertram had no faith, he needed his Uncle Jacob, who was a man of faith, to answer it for him. So Bertram set up his machine, adjusted the settings, and went in search of his uncle to have the question answered.

CHAPTER 8

THE TEST FOR FAITH

Bertram directed Jacob to view the machine with a deliberate wave of his right hand. He put an added flourish into the gesture to be certain that Jacob had seen the red enamel ring on his finger. Then Bertram stepped aside and stood to the right of his machine. Jacob, seeing the flash of red as it passed before him, said, "That's an unusual ring. I've never seen you wear it before. Is it part of the test?"

"Yes. It is."

"What does it do?"

"The answer to that question will be revealed to you at a later time," Bertram said.

"Oh? Why is that?"

"Consider it a mystery; one of those things in real-life that you see, but don't really understand completely, like the sun or the stars. It's something I call Amoral Deceit."

"Amoral Deceit? That's a new one. When did you come up with that? As far as I know, deceit is always a sin."

Bertram said, "Amoral Deceit means that sometimes things just happen. They're neither good nor bad. They just happen, by chance."

"Things don't just happen by chance, Bertram. You know that. Everything happens for a reason. It's all part of God's Plan. Right?"

"I know. What I mean is that it's like with Moses and the people who lived back then. They believed that the sun revolved around the Earth, but later on, we found out that they were wrong. By Amoral Deceit, I mean that it wasn't evil for them to be deceived about believing that the sun was revolving around the Earth. It was just a mistake. But if it's like you say, and nothing happens by chance, then I guess that means that God must have deliberately tricked them into believing that the sun was revolving around the Earth?"

"I think that there's something else that you've forgotten, Bertram. God is responsible for all that is good. And Satan is responsible for all that is evil. It is Satan who clouds our perception so that we cannot see the truth, not God."

"Okay, but then why didn't God come down from Heaven and tell them the truth? Instead He just allowed Satan to continue to deceive them into believing a lie."

"What else is God to do, Bertram? Do you think that God should come down from Heaven and personally tell you every time that Satan tries to deceive you? That's not the way it works. God wants us to seek Him out, not the other way around. But go on," Jacob said. "I'm sorry. I didn't mean to interrupt you with a sermon."

Jacob looked towards Bertram's faith machine. "I must say, all of this stuff does look very interesting. Did you build it?"

"Yes."

"What does it do?"

"It's a machine that creates faith so that I can study it," Bertram said. "At least that's what I'm hoping it will do."

"Hm, and how does it do that?"

"Learning about how it does it is part of the test," Bertram said. "Go on. Take a look at it. Tell me what you think, but please don't touch anything."

"Why? Is it dangerous?"

"No. I just don't want you to accidentally knock anything out of place. It might ruin the results of the test."

"Oh, okay," Jacob said. "Don't worry, I promise. I'll be careful. I won't touch a thing." Jacob continued his examination of the machine as Bertram looked on, watching him carefully to make sure that he didn't do anything that might spoil the test. Jacob stepped around the machine slowly, hands behind his back, viewing it from various angles as he did so, and after a thorough examination, Jacob determined that Bertram's faith machine was little more than a post, a battery, and a bucket with Christmas tree lights. Finally he said to his nephew, "So what do you call it? A Grav-o-meter?"

"No, it's a Gra-vom-eter, like the way you say thermometer."

"Oh? I thought it was supposed to have something to do with faith?" Jacob said.

"It does. It tests for faith by using the Earth's gravitational field."

"Interesting. How does that work?"

Bertram said, "It's not my intention to prove or to disprove the existence of God. I want to study faith in a clinical setting to see how it works, but in order to do that, I need the help of the people I'm testing. I need to know what they're thinking and why they're thinking it.

"And the only way I can know that is to ask them, but if my questions make them feel like I'm ridiculing their religious beliefs, they might become resentful and refuse to finish the test or purposely choose to give me false answers. Either way, the experiment would be a failure, and I would not find out what I wanted to know.

"To keep that from happening," Bertram said, "I decided that it might be best to study a less controversial kind of faith, one that didn't inspire such strong emotional reactions when I began questioning it, and fortunately, people have faith in all sorts of things that they can't see besides God. So I built this machine," Bertram said. "It tests for the faith that people have in gravity. I've noticed that people don't seem to get too upset when you start questioning their faith in that."

"No, they don't," Jacob said. "Very interesting. How does it work?"

"Like I said, learning how it works is part of the test."

"And what does that mean, exactly?" Jacob said.

"It means that I will eventually explain everything you need to know about the machine, but not all at once. You'll only learn about it bit by bit, because that's the way we learn things in real life, in pieces. And some things we never learn at all. It's this element of uncertainty, of not knowing, I believe, that causes faith to happen in some people. This test, with the help of my machine, will try to simulate those same conditions of uncertainty, and hopefully trigger the Faith Response in you so that I can observe it and take notes and learn from it."

This time Jacob had to smile. He said, "So your goal is to try to create simulated faith inside my brain, is that it?"

"In a manner of speaking, yes, but not simulated faith. I'm just simulating the conditions that I hope will cause the faith to happen. The faith should be real."

"How will you be able to tell?"

"I won't. That will be up to you. You're the expert. You know what real faith is like; I don't. That's why maintaining an honest rapport with my test subject is so important. The Faith Event, if it does occur, won't be happening inside my mind. It'll be happening inside yours, so if there is a difference, it'll be up to you to feel it and to tell me if it's real or not."

"I see," Jacob said. He smiled again.

"Is something wrong, Father?"

"No. Well...it's just that this whole thing seems a little...absurd to me."

"I'm glad you think so," Bertram said. "I've always felt that when dealing with the unknown that a little skepticism is a good thing. 'Test everything. Hold on to the good.' Right? So, shall we begin?"

"I'm ready if you are."

"Good. Then I will proceed," Bertram said and he stepped in front of Jacob and took a position to the right of his machine. "As I mentioned earlier," Bertram said, "the process by which you will learn about the machine's operation is meant to duplicate the way we learn things in real life, and as we so often discover in real life, the things we think we know and understand, aren't always so.

"To simulate this," Bertram said, "I've broken down the information that you will be taught into a series of lessons. Each lesson will be followed by a set of predictions that you will be required to make to test your faith in The Law of Gravity and to test your understanding of the machine's design."

"What if you're a lousy teacher?"

"That's a good point, Father. I might be, but then aren't many of the decisions we have to make in real life based on bad information given to us by 'lousy teachers' or biased news agencies? It will be up to you to determine what to believe and what not to believe, but I will promise you this: I will never knowingly tell you a lie, though sometimes I will withhold certain facts from you and allow you to draw your own conclusions."

"Like the ring?"

"Yes," Bertram said, "the ring is one example. There'll be others as the experiment progresses, most not as obvious as the ring, but you'll see what I mean once you become more familiar with the process. The point I'm trying to make here is that my intention in withholding these facts is not to try to trick you into making a wrong prediction, but to try to simulate those mysteries in real life for which there seem to be no answers. Things like: 'What does an electron really look like?' or 'Why doesn't God show Himself the way He used to in The Old Testament?'

"You see Father, that's another one of my theories about faith, that without mystery and uncertainty, faith could not be possible; and since it's my goal to somehow artificially create faith in your mind, I must first create an artificial mystery to inspire it. It is my hope that if I can understand the way your mind works, the way it deals with mystery, then maybe I can somehow learn to recreate those same thought processes within my own mind, and one day have faith too, just like you do."

"Bertram," Jacob said, "faith is not something we learn. It's a gift given to us by the Grace of God. You can't acquire it through science or manufacture it in a machine, and even if you could, it wouldn't be real. Faith has to come from the heart."

"I don't see why it should matter where it comes from, only that I have it."

"You wouldn't want to sell your soul to the Devil in exchange for a place in Heaven. Would you?"

"I wonder if that's possible?" Bertram said.

"May I ask you a question, Son?"

"Yes. What is it?"

"If you are seriously convinced that it might be possible to create faith using this machine, have you considered testing it on yourself first to see what happens?"

"Yes, I have. But it won't work on me."

"Why? Because you believe you have no faith?"

"No, because I built the machine. I know everything about it. For me, there is no mystery in it. And without mystery, faith cannot exist. That's my theory, remember? And if I'm right it begs a larger question, doesn't it? Since God made everything in existence and has Absolute Knowledge of all things, does that mean that He too is incapable of having faith?"

"We are made in God's image," Jacob said. "I think it's reasonable to conclude that since we have faith, then God must have faith too."

"Yes, I suppose that's another possibility. Sorry, I didn't mean to get off track. This is an experiment to test faith, not God."

"You do keep saying that," Jacob said. "Are you sure?"

Bertram smiled and redirected Jacob's attention back to the machine. "This will be your first lesson," he said and he demonstrated to Jacob the operation of the Black Box. He opened the lid to let Jacob look inside and he flipped the latch to activate the trapdoor. When Bertram was done with this demonstration, he asked Jacob if he had any questions.

Jacob said, "Yes. I do."

"What is it?"

Jacob pointed to the switch that hung from the picture hook by a string, the switch labeled Test Switch. "What does this switch do?" he said. "It's not connected to anything. It's just hanging on a string. How does it work?"

Bertram said, "The operation of the Test Switch will be revealed to you at a later time. I promise."

"Ah, more of your amoral deceit?"

"Yes. Do you have any other questions?"

"No. Not for now."

"Then it's time to make your first prediction."

"What am I to predict?"

"The future, of course," Bertram said, and he reached into the bucket and removed the three items from within it, the blue Ping-Pong ball, the plastic croquet ball, and the shiny black stone. He gave both of the balls to Jacob so that he could inspect them, but kept the stone for himself. Bertram said, "You will now be required to predict what will happen to this stone once I put it inside of the Black Box, and later, flip the latch on the trapdoor."

"That's easy enough," Jacob said. "The trapdoor will open and the stone will fall into the bucket...providing there're no tricks."

"There're no tricks," Bertram said.

"Then the stone will fall into the bucket."

"You're certain of that?"

"Yes."

"Then I will proceed," Bertram said. He closed the trapdoor on the Black Box, and with his left hand, placed the stone inside of the box. He placed his fingertips on the latch to the trapdoor and prepared to activate it. "Any last minute changes in your prediction?"

"No. The stone will fall into the bucket."

"Okay then," Bertram said and he flipped the latch. The trapdoor opened and the stone fell into the bucket below.

"There, you see? You were right. It's as simple as that," Bertram said. "You understand how the machine works and you have faith in the Law of Gravity."

"So it would seem."

"You seem surprised."

"I must admit that I had been expecting some kind of trick."

"This is science Father, not magic. There are no tricks."

Bertram removed a small notepad from his back pocket and began to write in it. "What are you doing now?" Jacob said.

"I'm just recording the results of the first test."

"Oh."

When Bertram had finished making his entry into the notepad, he said, "Now if you would please hand me the larger of the two plastic balls I gave you earlier, we can proceed to your next prediction."

"I thought there was supposed to be another lesson first."

"Not always. It varies."

"Oh, okay," Jacob said and offered Bertram the ball. "It's that uncertainty thing you were talking about?"

"Yes," Bertram said, putting his hand out for the croquet ball, but stopping just as his fingertips came within reach. "Before I take it, though, is there anything that you'd like to know about it? Do you have any questions concerning it or the machine?"

"No, I don't think so. You've said that there'll be no tricks, and until you've proven otherwise, I will believe you."

"Then I will proceed," Bertram said and he closed and latched the trapdoor on the box. He took the crocquet ball from Jacob with his left hand and placed it inside of the Black Box and closed the lid. "Now you must make your next prediction. What will happen this time when I flip the latch and the trapdoor opens?"

"The trapdoor will open and the ball will fall into the bucket, of course."

"You're certain of that?"

"Yes."

"Okay, then I will proceed," Bertram said and he flipped the latch on the Black Box. The trapdoor opened but the ball did not fall from the box. It stayed inside.

Jacob was not surprised. "So what's the trick?" he said.

"It's not a trick," Bertram said. "If you look more closely at the Black Box, you will see that it's not a perfect cube. See it? The box tapers slightly from the top of the box to the bottom, so that the top of the box is slightly wider than the bottom of the box. The ball is small enough to fit in through the top, but not small enough to fall out through the bottom."

Bertram lifted the lid, so that Jacob could look inside the box. "Yes, I see that now," Jacob said. "I thought you said that there'd be no tricks."

"It's not a trick."

"It seems like a trick to me."

"But it isn't," Bertram said. "I admit that it is deceiving, but it's not a trick. If you had been more observant you might have noticed how the box tapered, but you didn't. It's just like the people back in Moses' time. They didn't notice how all of the stars in the sky weren't really staying in the same place.

"The stars looked like they were staying in the same place all the time," Bertram said, "but actually each star was going around and around in little egg-shaped circles. This is because the Earth goes around the sun in an egg-shaped circle. If anyone had noticed this back then, they might have begun to realize that the Earth was not standing still...just as you might have realized that the croquet ball was too big to fall through the bottom of the Black Box, if you had looked more closely at it.

"It's the same thing," Bertram said. "This machine is kind of like the universe. The facts are here for you to find or not to find, and if you do find them, to believe or not to believe, just as they are in the real world. Again, this is not a test to see how many predictions you get right or wrong. It's an experiment to try to understand why you make the choices that you make, to understand how you think. There are no right or wrong predictions. There are no right or wrong answers."

Jacob smiled. "If you say so, Son."

"It's true."

"And I believe you."

"Good," Bertram said. "Then I have one more prediction for you to make before we go on to the next step, but first I need you to give me the blue Ping-Pong ball...unless you have any questions about it?"

"As a matter of fact, I do," Jacob said. He was holding the blue Ping-Pong ball in his right hand, rolling it back and forth, from fingertip to fingertip, with his thumb. "I noticed that the larger ball is made out of a softer kind of plastic than this one, almost like vinyl. It gave more, when I squeezed it. But this one is more rigid. It hardly flexes at all when I squeeze it. Is there a reason for that?"

"Very good, Father. I have to say, you are getting much better at asking questions."

"I had a good teacher."

"Thank you Father—but to answer your question—is there a reason? Yes, there is. Ideally, I wanted both balls to be the same in every way except in size. Only I didn't have anything like that, so I had to settle for what I could find. The larger ball is actually part of a plastic croquet set for small children. I got it at a garage sale for ten cents. The ball you're holding now is a white Ping-Pong ball painted blue."

"Why did you paint it blue?"

"To match the larger ball. As I said, I wanted both balls to be the same in every way except size, and since the only thing I could find at the stores were white Ping-Pong balls, I had to paint this one blue."

"Or you could have painted the larger ball white?"

"Yes, I could have."

"But you didn't."

"No."

"Why is that?"

"Again, another excellent question," Bertram said. "But I'm afraid you'll have to wait for the answer to that one. To tell you now might ruin the outcome of the test."

"But there is a reason?"

"Yes."

"Then maybe I should have a closer look."

"Certainly," Bertram said. "I don't want your predictions to be compromised because you feel like you're being rushed into making a decision. Take your time. Ask as many questions as you like. There's no hurry."

"Okay," Jacob said and he held the Ping-Pang ball up to the ceiling lamp, studying it as he rolled it back and forth between his thumb and index finger. When everything appeared normal, he put the ball to his ear and shook it vigorously, listening as he did so, for some telltale sound that might betray some hidden secret inside, but he heard nothing suspicious. When he felt he had done all he could do to the ball, short of cutting the ball open with his pocket knife or mashing it flat, he gave it back to Bertram. "I guess I'm ready to proceed," he said.

"Very well," Bertram said. He closed the trapdoor on the Black Box, removed the plastic croquet ball, and with his left hand, replaced it with the blue Ping-Pong ball. "What will happen now, when I flip the latch and the trapdoor opens?" Bertram said.

"Could you open the lid so I can look inside?"

"Yes, there. How's that?"

"Better," Jacob said, inspecting the inside of the box. "Well this ball is much smaller than the other one, and it doesn't appear to be jammed up against the sides," Jacob said, "so I'd have to say that it will probably fall into the bucket, just like the stone did."

"You don't sound so sure. You're not losing your faith in gravity are you?"

"No. I still believe in gravity."

"Then it must be your trust in me? Maybe you still think I'm trying to trick you?"

"No. I trust you."

"Then why are you so uncertain?"

"You're right. I should be more certain. Let me rephrase that—I am absolutely sure that the ball will fall into the bucket when you open the trapdoor."

"Good," Bertram said, and he flipped the latch on the Black Box. The trapdoor opened and the Ping-Pong ball fell from the box and into the bucket below. It struck the tin bottom of the bucket with a resounding clack, rattled noisily against the insides of the bucket for a few seconds, and eventually settled into silence. Bertram allowed the silence to endure for a few more seconds so as to mark the end of the event. Then he pulled out his pencil and his notepad and recorded the result into his log.

When he had finished writing, he said, "This concludes the first phase of the experiment. We have seen how the Gravometer works when the power is turned off. Now we will see how it works with the power turned on."

PHASE TWO

"It's time for your next lesson," Bertram said. He pointed to a switch that was attached to the vertical post, a switch that was labeled ON/OFF SWITCH. "This is the Power Switch to the Gravometer. As the name implies, it turns The Gravometer on and off. It's what's known as a toggle switch. If I press it at the top, it turns The Gravometer on. If I press it at the bottom, it turns The Gravometer off. Notice that the switch is currently at its ON position and yet The Gravometer is off. Look." Bertram pressed the bottom part of the switch. It clicked as he reset it. "Now the switch is off and The Gravometer is still off. And even if I click the top part of the switch to turn it on, the Gravometer still stays off. See?"

"Yes."

"Watch," Bertram said. He clicked the Power Switch back and forth several times, turning the switch on and off in rapid succession. "See, the Gravometer never comes on."

"Okay. I see that. So how do you turn it on?"

"The machine will turn on only if I press the Start Button and the On/Off Switch at the same time. Here, let me show you." Bertram did so, and the blue Christmas tree lights taped around the bucket lit up and began to flash.

"The Gravometer has now been activated," Bertram said. "Do you have any questions?"

"No, I don't think so. It all looks pretty much the same except for the Christmas tree lights flashing on the bucket, and I don't think those should have any affect on gravity."

"Then it's time for your next prediction," Bertram said and he reached into the bucket with his left hand to retrieve the blue Ping-Pong ball. He placed the ball, using his left hand, inside the Black Box and he said, "With the machine on, what do you predict will happen this time, when the trapdoor opens?"

"I'm not really sure?"

"Oh? Why not? You just said that you didn't think flashing Christmas tree lights would have any affect on gravity."

"Yes, but I was thinking about what happened with the croquet ball. I didn't look close enough to notice how it was too big to fall through the bottom of the box, and now you have electricity running through this, uh,

Gravometer, so I really don't know what's going to happen next when you open the trapdoor."

"How very scientific of you, Father."

"Thank you, I guess."

"So what's your prediction then?"

"I guess I'm going to have to say that I don't really know what's going to happen when you flip the latch and the trapdoor opens."

"Very good, Father. 'I don't know,' is a valid response. I feel that too many people these days don't say 'I don't know' as often as they should. They just pretend that they 'do know' and then try to figure out what they're doing, while they're doing it."

"I agree. Many politicians and some religious leaders are often guilty of that very offense," Jacob said. "So, since I haven't got a clue as to what's going to happen when you open the trapdoor, why don't you just do it now, and we can both see what happens together?"

"Very well," Bertram said. He flipped the latch. The trapdoor opened, but nothing fell from the box. The Ping-Pong ball remained inside.

Jacob was not surprised. He said, "Yes, I was fairly certain something like that was going to happen."

"Then why didn't you say so?"

"Because I would have been guessing, not predicting. Predicting comes from understanding various scientific principles and applying them to real-life situations. And like I said, I don't understand any scientific principles about electricity."

Bertram smiled again. He said, "You know, Father, you are really beginning to sound more and more like a scientist."

"Or maybe I'm just beginning to sound more and more like you?"

"Maybe that's it," Bertram said, and he gave his uncle a sly grin.

"What's next?"

"Next I will show you why the ball did not fall from the Black Box when the trapdoor opened. Come closer, take a look," Bertram said. He lifted the lid on the Black Box and invited Jacob to look inside. When Jacob looked into the box, he saw that the blue Ping-Pong ball was stuck to the inside back wall of the Black Box.

Bertram reached into the box and pinched the Ping-Pong ball until it was no longer touching the back wall, just a fraction of an inch. Then he released the ball and it sprang from his fingertips, as if by some unseen force, and reattached itself to the back wall. He did this again so that Jacob could be sure to see what was happening.

"Static electricity?" Jacob said.

"No. An electromagnet. It's inside the post behind the Black Box. It turns on at the same time that the Christmas tree lights come on. They're both connected to the same circuit."

"Oh? So there's a magnet inside the post?"

"Yes," Bertram said. "The post is actually hollow inside. In fact, it's not even a real post. It's really four separate plywood panels nailed together to give the appearance of a solid post. What really makes it look convincing is this piece here, on top. I cut the end off of a real post and used it as a cap to make it look solid. A little wood putty, some sanding, a good layer of paint, and you really can't tell the difference. What do you think?"

"I'm impressed. Maybe you should think about becoming a carpenter instead of a scientist."

"Thank you, Father, but I don't think so," Bertram said and he showed his uncle the purple-blue thumbnail on his left hand.

"Ouch. How'd you do that?"

"By being a very bad carpenter."

"Oh."

"Any way, I'd originally planned on—"

"Excuse me for interrupting, but did you say an electromagnet?"

"Yes."

"Where did you find an electromagnet?"

"I found most of the parts I needed from TV sets, washing machines, and other stuff that people put out by the road for the garbage men to take away."

"Very clever, but how does a magnet attract a Ping-Pong ball? Magnets are only supposed to attract things that are made out of metal."

"It isn't an ordinary Ping-Pong ball. I had to carefully slice it open with a razor blade so that I could insert a set of very thin curved iron plates, and then glue it back together again—which is, by the way, that other reason I'd mentioned earlier."

"What other reason?"

"The other reason I chose to paint the Ping-Pong ball blue instead of painting the croquet ball white. Remember you asked me that question?"

"Oh, yes."

"Painting the Ping-Pong ball blue also helped to hide the place where I cut it."

"Bertram," Jacob said. "You seem to make a distinction between withholding the truth and outright telling a lie, as if one were more morally correct than the other. Tell me, Son, is that what you really believe?"

"No, I believe that morality is dependent on intent. Withholding the truth and telling a lie can both be moral acts if the intent is to do good, just as telling the truth can be an immoral act if the intent is to cause harm. And if the act neither helps nor harms then it is neither good nor evil. It is amoral. I believe that truth is like that. Truth is neither moral nor immoral. It simply exists and we try to understand it."

"That's where we disagree, Son. Creation is good. Genesis, Chapter One, remember? God looked at what He had created and saw that it was good. Physical Truth arises from Creation and if Creation is good, then Truth must also be good. There is no such thing as amorality."

"What about 'one plus one equals two?' That's a kind of truth," Bertram said. "A universal mathematical truth. Tell me, how is that good or evil?"

"It is good," Jacob said, "because it is the foundation of modern-day mathematics and physical science which, if understood properly, can help to better the lives of people and their families, and ease the burden of human suffering."

"And gravity. How is that good or evil?"

"It is good because it allows life to exist on this planet. Without it, Creation, as we know it, could not exist."

"And when someone jumps off a building to commit suicide and is pulled to his death by the Earth's gravitational field, how is that good?"

"That is why God put down a set of rules for men to live by...Tempt not The Lord thy God. Remember?"

"So every time I pick up a ball and let it fall from my hand to the Earth, that is a moral act?"

"Yes, because it's falling is a result of Moral Principles."

"But if that's true, then you must agree that it is also a form of deceit."

"Why?"

"Because we don't understand *why* it falls. The knowledge of why it falls is being withheld from us, just as I am withholding knowledge from you about this machine."

"I agree, but that still doesn't make it amoral. If anything, it is either moral or immoral deceit. Yes, I agree with you, Son. We *are* being deceived about gravity, but who is deceiving us? If God is deceiving us, it is moral. If Satan is deceiving us, it is immoral. It's as simple as that."

"Because everything happens for a reason?"

"Yes."

"Then what about Newton's Law?"

"What about it?"

"The two forces, equal and opposite reactions, good and evil, remember?"

"I thought we already covered that; God is responsible for the good action and Satan is responsible for the evil reaction. Remember?"

"Yes, of course."

Jacob said, "It's clear to me now that you and I see the same universe in a very different way. To you, it is a mysterious place full of question marks and contradictions, where a pair of dice rolled onto a tabletop is a random act that is neither good nor evil. Or maybe to you it's both, so they cancel each other out. To you, it's what men do with the dice that creates morality, because to you, morality is a thought process or an emotional reaction that exists only within the human mind. But to me, Bertram, morality is something greater than myself. Morality is of God."

"But if that's what you believe," Bertram said, "then you must also believe that even the tiniest vibration of a single atom must carry with it some kind of moral quality?"

"Yes! That's exactly what I believe."

Bertram thought about this for a while. "I see," he said quietly.

"I hope that doesn't spoil your theories and ruin the rest of your experiment."

"No," Bertram said, "Not at all. It just makes the test even more interesting than it was before. Are you ready to proceed?"

"Yes, I am. But I would like to see that Ping-Pong ball again, if that's permitted...to see what I missed."

"Sure," Bertram said and he reached into the Black Box and gave the ball back to Jacob. Jacob took it and reexamined it to see if he could find the place where it had been cut and the iron plates inserted, but the surface appeared unblemished.

"You did a good job," he said.

"Thank you. I ruined eight other Ping-Pong balls before I got it right. Is there anything else you'd like to see before we continue?"

"No, I don't think so."

"Good. Then we can proceed," Bertram said and he put his hand out for the ball.

But Jacob didn't give it to him. "Would it be permissible for me to place the Ping-Pong ball into the box this time?" Jacob said.

"No, I'm afraid not. The procedure by which I conduct the experiment requires that I alone place objects into the Black Box."

"Why is that?"

"Because I am the expert on the machine. You are not. You must trust me to work the machine for you, just as you are required to trust those elected officials in government to work the political machine on your behalf. The Israelites were expected to trust Aaron's sons to take their offerings to the altar on their behalf, because they were not qualified by God to do it themselves. It's the same thing."

"Faith, I've noticed, seems to have a lot to do with trust," Bertram said, "trusting people who claim to know what God is thinking. God 'spoke' only to the prophets. Everyone else was expected to trust them and to believe them because they supposedly knew what God was thinking."

"Yes, that is true, Son. God chooses certain men as prophets to preach His message to the world, men like Moses and the Apostle Paul. They were men of God, and we, as people of God, must trust them to speak for God."

"And that's all I'm asking of you, Father. Do you trust me?" Bertram said.

"To speak for God?"

"No," Bertram laughed. "Just to place the ball into the box for you."

"Yes, Son, I think I can trust you for that," Jacob said, and he placed the ball into Bertram's hand.

Bertram took the ball, closed the trapdoor, and with his left hand placed the Ping-Pong ball inside of the Black Box. He shut the lid and reached down and pressed the bottom part of the On/Off Switch to turn The Gravometer off. The switch clicked and the flashing Christmas tree lights around the bucket went out. "With The Gravometer off," Bertram said, "what do you predict will happen this time, when I flip the latch on the trapdoor?"

"This one's easy," Jacob said. "It's just like the first time. The Gravometer is off, so the ball must fall into the bucket, of course."

"You're certain of that?"

"Yes—no. Wait," Jacob said. "Was the On/Off Switch 'on' the first time we did it this way, or was it 'off?' I can't remember..."

"So what's your prediction?"

"Hmm, I don't really know, sorry. It's a little confusing."

"You know," Bertram said. "You're right. It is a little confusing. No problem, I think I see where I went wrong. When I first came up with the idea, it all seemed pretty clear to me, but now I see, explaining it to myself is easier than explaining it to someone else. So why don't I just clarify things before we move on to the next step?"

"Sounds good to me. It's your experiment. I'm just a lab rat."

Bertram flipped the latch on the trapdoor and the Ping-Pong ball fell out of the Black Box and into the bucket. He closed the trapdoor again, put the Ping-Pong ball back into the Black Box with his left hand again, and he said, "Do you feel any faith forming in your mind now?"

"Sorry," Jacob said. "No."

"Don't worry, we'll work through it," Bertram said and he flipped the latch on the Black Box and the Ping-Pong ball fell out of the box again. "Feel any faith forming in your mind now?" he said.

Jacob shook his head, "No."

"No problem," Bertram said. "It only proves my point. There's no mystery involved in the falling of the Ping-Pong ball. That's why the faith hasn't started forming in your mind yet."

"Oh, okay. If you say so."

"But you don't believe it?"

"Faith comes from God, Bertram, not from a machine."

"The machine doesn't make faith. It inspires it."

"What's that supposed to mean?"

"It means that now we add some mystery to the process and we see what happens. Remember the Test Switch? You asked me what it tested and how it could work if it wasn't connected to anything?"

"Yes."

"The reason it doesn't need to be connected to anything in order for it to work is because the thing that it tests for is Faith."

Jacob smiled with interest. "How does it do that?"

"You're about to find out. It's time for your next prediction," Bertram said. He reached into the bucket with his right hand to retrieve the Ping-Pong ball. He closed the trapdoor on the Black Box with his left hand.

Bertram placed the Ping-Pong ball inside the Black Box with his right hand, and while his hand was still inside the box, he made a fist and lightly touched the magnet ring on his finger to the ball. When he felt the ball attach itself to the ring, he removed his hand from the box, fingers together, so that Jacob could see his palm, but not the Ping-Pong ball attached to the ring on the backside of his hand. Bertram closed the lid on the empty box with his left hand and he said, "What do you predict will happen this time, when I flip the latch and the trapdoor opens?"

"The ball will fall into the bucket, of course."

"You're certain of that?"

"Yes, absolutely certain."

"You are certain because there is no mystery in it now, nothing has changed."

"No. I am certain of it because I have faith in The Law of Gravity and I have trust in you to be an honest person."

"But what if I do this?" Bertram said, and taking the Test Switch that hung from the string into his left hand, he pressed it with his thumb. It clicked into place as he did so. "There now," Bertram said. "The switch is on. What is your prediction now? Is it the same, or has it changed?" Bertram released the switch and let it hang, as it had before, from the picture hook by the string. "Do you still believe that the ball will fall out of the box once the trapdoor opens? Or do you believe that something else will happen now?"

"I don't see how this proves anything."

"No? Then what's your prediction?"

"How should I know? You've changed the conditions of the test."

"No, not really. You've said yourself, there's no way that the switch can work because it's not connected to anything; it's just hanging from a string. How could turning it on or off change the conditions of the test?"

"As I've said before, I don't know very much about electricity. Maybe this Test Switch works on a principle that I am not familiar with," Jacob said.

"But you do know that string does not conduct electricity."

"Yes, but I also know that TV remotes work without strings or without being connected to anything either, so maybe you're using this Test Switch as a kind of remote control to turn on the magnet?"

"Yes, I suppose that's possible, but it isn't. And you can know for certain that it isn't too."

"How?"

"Because I give you my word that it isn't. You have admitted that you don't know very much about electricity, so your doubt is understandable. To you, it is a mystery, but to me it is not, because I am the expert of this machine. I built it. I know everything about it, and you can know everything about it too, if you trust me, if you believe what I tell you."

"I see," Jacob said.

"So before you make your final prediction official, I will tell you a truth about The Test Switch, and it will be up to you to believe it or to not believe it. And the truth that I will tell you is this: The Test Switch is not a remote and the string is just a string. It will not conduct electricity."

Jacob was quiet for a moment, and then he said, "I think I see now."

"What?"

"How your machine works."

"Then you should have no problem making your prediction."

"But it isn't about predictions, is it Bertram? Or gravity. It's about you and me. And trust. You've asked me to trust you, as I have always expected you to trust me about what I know of God. But if I trust you and I'm proven wrong, then you may think that maybe I'm wrong about God too, because my knowledge is based on trusting the people who wrote The Bible. But if I don't trust you, then why should I ever expect you to trust me about the things I tell you about God? That's it, isn't it?"

Bertram said, "It's not that I don't trust you, Father. I do. You're the one person in the world that I do trust, but you don't have Absolute Knowledge of God. No one does. You only know what you think you believe is true. You didn't write the Bible. You didn't build The Church. Other people did. You only have their word that any of it is true.

"I, on the other hand, do have Absolute knowledge of this machine, because I built it. And yet, you can believe the people who wrote the Bible more than you can believe me. What a strange thing faith is; it can cause you to believe in people that you've never met, but not in the people that you know."

"I thought I knew you, Bertram, but now I'm not so sure..."

"Why? Have I ever lied to you?"

"I don't know. Have you?"

"That depends. Were you lying to me when you secretly paid Billy for his grades without telling me about it?"

"Yes," Jacob said. "I suppose I was, in a way, but I did that to protect you. I didn't want to see you or Billy hurt."

"If that is a lie, Father, then, yes. I have lied to you too," Bertram said. "When Billy and I were in school together, I led you to believe that I was no better at schoolwork than he was. The truth is, I could have always brought home straight "A" report cards if I'd wanted to. I simply chose not to because I knew that it would have been wrong. I know how love is. I've seen it. I know how it can cause people to do terrible things. I saw how much Billy wanted and needed your love.

"It would have been wrong for me to outshine Billy in school and cause him to do something hurtful because he felt that I had shamed him in your eyes. You had been kind enough to take me into your home. For me to disregard that kindness by harming Billy in that way would have been, to me, immoral."

"You did that...for him?"

"Yes."

"I'm sorry. I didn't know," Jacob said, and then he understood what it was that God was wanting him to do and he knew that to deny Bertram his trust would only crush the fragile measure of faith that God had, for some reason, chosen to give him. But Jacob also knew that to give Bertram his trust now, and then go on to make a wrong prediction because of it, would only prove Bertram's Hypothesis and cause Bertram to lose faith in another way. Either choice he could make would lead Jacob to the same trap.

And so Jacob did the only thing that he knew would save both Bertram and himself. He had *faith* that God would use him in such a way to make his meaning clear, for this had been God's plan all along, to show Bertram the true meaning of faith and to, ultimately, save his immortal soul.

"Is something the matter, Father?"

"No," Jacob said. "You're right. You have never given me a reason to distrust you. You've always been honest and truthful with me. Why should I doubt your character now? So my prediction will remain unchanged. When the trapdoor opens, the ball will fall into the bucket." And to prove his point, Jacob reached out to the Black Box to flip the latch himself, but Bertram stopped him before he could.

It had been Bertram's intention to open the trapdoor himself, but doing so now seemed wrong somehow. It was odd. Despite all of his careful planning and all of his talk of amorality, somehow morality had managed to seep in anyway, and he couldn't ignore it.

"Is something wrong, Son?" Jacob said.

"No, Father. The test is over, that's all. Faith is about believing, not about knowing. Remember? It's not important to know what the truth is, only that you believe it's true."

Jacob said, "Is that what you think faith is all about, Bertram? Believing in something whether it's true or not? Faith is more than that. It's about believing in something and *knowing* that it's true."

"How do you do that?" Bertram said.

Jacob smiled. "There isn't anything inside the box, is there, Son?"

"No," Bertram said, a smile forming on his lips, as he began to realize that he had been caught in his own trap. "There isn't," he said, "how did you know?"

"The same way I know that God is real and that Jesus is his Son," Jacob said, "Faith." Jacob reached past Bertram's hand and flipped the latch himself. The trapdoor opened and nothing fell out. The box was empty, just as Jacob had predicted.

Bertram had to laugh.

CHAPTER 9

Eliot Corbel was an Egotist and an Atheist. He loved himself for he was God. Sole Heir to the vast Corbel Railroad Fortune, Eliot put no other gods before himself or his desires. He had a chrome vanity plate installed on the grill of his European luxury sedan that read:

> I'M RICH
> UR NOT
> 2 BAD 4U!

His rationale behind this elevated opinion of himself was this: If God did exist, and if He did come down to Earth for a visit, wouldn't He set Himself up in the most luxurious surroundings? Surround Himself with the most interesting people? Arrange physical reality so that He would have the best house, the best car, the most comfortable bed, the finest food to eat, and an endless supply of monetary wealth so that He could spend His days enjoying all of the sensual pleasures that physical reality had to offer? Eliot thought so, because this was exactly the place that he found himself on the planet Earth, with enough money and power and leisure time to do with whatever he pleased.

Eliot fancied himself a Venture Capitalist, a Renaissance man, and an Entrepreneur, though the majority of his business dealings usually lost him money; this was of little concern to him. Eliot had enough wealth to last him a hundred lifetimes, so profit was not a motivating factor that prompted Eliot to enter into a business venture.

His primary goal in transacting business was to see how much pain and suffering he could inflict upon those people who were actually trying to start up and run a legitimate company. He found this entertaining, sometimes even ethical. Seeing a business venture fail because of his disruptive influence in it gave him a genuine sense of satisfaction. "Did we really need another gas station or another strip mall in the world?" he had been heard to say as justification for what he did.

It was during the course of one of these "business ventures" that led Eliot to find himself where he was today, holding a position as Dean of Philosophical Pursuits at The Florida School of Business Technology. As Dean, a self-appointed position that allowed Eliot to wander the campus with an air of authority without having to do any actual work, Eliot was free to do pretty much as he pleased as he waited to "cash-in" or to "cash-out" of the deal.

This left Eliot's buddies having to contend with all of the mundane tasks involved in actually running the school; working with the local governments, paying the taxes and the creditors, fixing all the things that broke down, and teaching the classes, or rather, giving the appearance of teaching the classes.

The school, which Eliot set up, was part of a land deal that was steadily beginning to sour. Eliot had acquired the land from the state at a price far below its actual market value on the condition that he set up a business that would help stimulate the rural economies of Taylor County in Northern Florida. Eliot sold the county on the idea of a Business College as a "cash cow" that would bring to the area a younger demographic eager to spend money given to them by their rich parents.

After the land had been cleared and portable buildings moved in, the deal sweetened when Eliot learned of a nation-wide supermarket chain that had taken an interest in the land. This had all of Eliot's rich buddies (who weren't near as rich as Eliot) admiring his business savvy and giving him the thumbs-up (for about a week) at the prospect of a quick "cash-out." But the deal fell apart, leaving Eliot and his buddies stuck, holding the property and the school.

Eliot's buddies were becoming increasingly disturbed by his lack of concern regarding their initial investment and annoyed by his stonewalling every time they wanted to know when they could expect to receive their profits from the deal. Mutiny was in the air and Eliot found himself having constantly to fill in for his buddies whenever they decided that they had had enough of the school and were tired of showing up to "teach" their classes.

It would be during a series of these classes when Eliot was substituting for one or another of his buddies, who had decided for any number of baseless reasons not to show up for work, that Eliot Corbel's life would become inextricably intertwined with the life of Bertram Grey.

CHAPTER 10

After graduating high school, Bertram wasted no time in sending out queries for scholarships to any good college that would have him, but his efforts were stymied by the low grade point average he had acquired while keeping his grades low to make Billy's grades look better. Bertram did, however, receive one favorable response from a facility of higher learning, a college called The Florida School of Business Technology.

One week after receiving his letter of acceptance, guaranteeing him to receive the necessary funds through student loans and government grants, Bertram decided to take a bus to Florida to tour the campus to see what the school had to offer. He was somewhat disappointed to find that the school was more "business" than "technology," but he figured that the laws of mathematics and the laws of physics were the same no matter where they were taught—either there or at some prestigious college with a high sounding name. And since he had received no offers from any of those kinds of establishments, Bertram signed the papers and registered to begin class during the fall semester.

When Bertram returned home, his Aunt Elizabeth surprised him with a special meal to celebrate. She had all of his favorites: fried eggplant with baked potatoes and sour cream, cornbread with green beans and field peas, and apple pie with vanilla ice cream for dessert. Bertram had second helpings of everything and third helpings of pie. Afterwards, they went out on the front porch to enjoy the evening and to watch the sunset.

"Thank you for the dinner, Mother. It was very nice," Bertram said.

"You're very welcome, Son. It was no trouble. We're very proud of you." Her tone was pleasant, but anxious. "When do you think you'll be leaving?" she said.

"In August."

"So soon?"

"Yes. I've already signed up."

"I was hoping you'd be here for Christmas."

"I'll drop in. It's only about a day's drive from there to here."

"You don't have a car."

"I'll catch a bus. Don't worry. I'll get here somehow."

"Don't hitch-hike."

"I won't."

"Good, we'll be expecting you—for Thanksgiving too."

"I'll be here. I promise."

"You'd better, or I'll be driving down there myself to get you."

Bertram smiled at the idle threat. He knew that she never drove more than five miles from her doorstep and was rarely in her car for more than twenty minutes at a time, which was all the driving she could really handle. Fortunately, this was never a problem for her, because everything she ever wanted or needed was safely within the town limits of Pietyville and there was never a reason for her to have to travel further.

"I'll be here," Bertram said again. "I promise. Please, don't do anything rash."

"Good then, I'm glad that's settled," she said and she rose from the front porch swing and gave Bertram a hug, but broke away suddenly and rushed back into the house, because she said that she had forgotten to put the ice cream in the freezer and she didn't want it to melt.

Bertram started to follow her, but Jacob stopped him. "She'll be fine," he said. "She just doesn't like good-byes."

Bertram said, "I know. Neither do I."

When August did arrive, more quickly than Bertram imagined it would, he packed his things together and Jacob took him to the bus stop alone. His Aunt Elizabeth had intended to go with them, but she got busy in the kitchen cooking a meal for a friend who had suddenly taken ill. When the time came for them to leave, she still had a casserole in the oven and couldn't leave it unattended. Bertram said he understood, and she kissed him lightly on the cheek, hugged him one long last time, and released him to the world with a brown paper sack full of warm cookies.

"Well I guess we're off," Jacob said to Bertram from the driver's seat of his car.

"I guess so," Bertram said.

"A little nervous?"

Bertram smiled, "No, not really."

"Good. I'm sure you'll do just fine."

Bertram turned to look out of the passenger side window to the porch of the old house, one last time, and saw his Aunt Elizabeth standing alone, near the porch swing, watching them. "You be sure to phone me as soon as you get there," she called out to him. Bertram promised that he would. They both waved goodbye to each other, but neither of them said it.

THE MORAL MACHINE

The bus depot was located just beyond a set of railroad tracks that marked the eastern edge of town. Because it was so close to the house they left only a few minutes before the bus was scheduled to depart, but a freight train on its way north with a load of pulp wood blocked their way and they had to wait for it to pass.

Bertram said, "I wonder if this is some kind of omen. Maybe something's trying to tell me I'm not supposed to leave."

"I didn't think you believed in that sort of thing. It's not very scientific."

"I know. It's just one of those things you think about sometimes, I guess. I don't really believe it—it's like that thing my mother used to tell me about trains. She used to tell me that it was bad luck to count the number of cars on a train as it passed by, because if you counted them all, then someone you knew would die."

"Your Mother Elizabeth told you that?"

"No, my real mother. Your sister, Gertrude."

"Oh? Funny, I don't remember her being superstitious like that, but you know, now that you mention it, I do seem to remember my own mother telling me something like that too. I'd almost forgotten it."

"Maybe that's where she heard it."

"Maybe so."

"Did you believe it?" Bertram said. "When she told you?"

"Like I said, I only just now remember her telling me about it, so it must not have made a big impression on me. I don't know. What about you? Did you believe it?"

"No."

"Not even at first?"

Bertram shook his head. "No. She told me about the trains right after I found out about Santa Claus and the Easter Bunny, so I was pretty skeptical after that. But just to be sure, I counted the number of cars on a train just to see what would happen."

"Even though you weren't sure?"

"Yes."

"Weren't you concerned that your test might cause someone to die if you were wrong?"

"No. Because I was fairly certain I was right."

"Why was that?"

Bertram said, "When I was a child, I noticed how grownups would put up signs to warn people about dangerous places and things, especially around train stations and railroad tracks, but I never saw any signs warning people not to count the number of cars on a train."

"How old were you then?" Jacob said.

"Eight or nine, I think."

"Eight or nine?"

"I think so."

"What a clever thing to notice at so young an age."

"I was always noticing things like that," Bertram said. "I guess I was made that way."

"Did you ever tell your mother what you did?"

"Yes, but I waited a while to make sure that no one was going to die by coincidence—and when no one did—that's when I told her."

"What did she say?"

"She just got very nervous and tried to make me promise not to do it again. I asked her why. She said that when she was a child, growing up, that she had a friend whose mother and father died suddenly—one in a car accident and the other of a heart attack. She said that both deaths happened right after someone had counted the number of cars on a train, so that proved it was true. 'What about the cars on the train that I had counted?' I asked her. No one we knew had died and that was over a month ago.

"She said the reason that no one had died was because I'd been lucky enough to have miscounted the cars. The curse only worked if you counted the number of cars on the train correctly and I had obviously counted them wrong, otherwise someone would have died.

"I was still kind of skeptical about it so I decided to try again, but this time I made sure that the train I counted was so short that there'd be no dispute as to whether I miscounted the cars or not."

"That was smart. Did it convince her?" Jacob said.

"No. Instead, she told me that the reason no one had died that time was because the train I had counted was too short—it only had six cars. She said that in order for the curse to work, it had to be a long train, long enough so you couldn't see the engine and the caboose at the same time. So from then on, I only counted long trains and I always used a pencil and a pad to mark down each car as it passed by to make sure that I didn't accidentally lose track and miscount them again."

"And did she finally believe you?"

"No, because every time I came to her with proof, she'd always come up with some new reason as to why the train I counted was invalid—either it was the wrong kind of train or the train had no caboose, or if it did have a caboose, it was the wrong color. The curse only worked on trains with red cabooses. It was always something."

"Yes, that's the way superstitions work, Bertram. People believe in them no matter what you try to tell them."

"It sounds kind of like having faith," Bertram said. "You believe in it no matter what other people try to tell you."

"It's not the same thing."

"Why?"

"A superstition is a misguided belief," Jacob said. "Sometimes people mistakenly believe they understand something about the way life works and they try to use that 'knowledge' to find happiness or to keep themselves, and the people they love, safe from harm. Sometimes what they believe sounds foolish—like counting the cars on a train. Other times it sounds more sensible—like counting on science and logic for answers. But either way, it's a false belief, based on false knowledge, because only faith in God can keep us safe and give us happiness."

Bertram listened; he neither agreed nor disagreed with his uncle.

Jacob said, "So, were you ever able to convince your mother that you were right and she was wrong?"

"No, and after awhile I just stopped trying. It only made her nervous and I could see I wasn't getting anywhere. She was going to believe what she wanted to believe no matter what I said or did. Besides, there were plenty of other things that she believed in that I didn't—things more important than trains—so I let it go."

"Yes, that's usually best," Jacob said. "Trying to force someone to believe a certain way usually only makes matters worse. All you can really do is pray for that person, and hope, one day that she or he will see The Light and allow God to come into his life."

"That's true," Bertram said. "You can't make a person believe anything he doesn't want to believe, even if what you want him to believe is the truth."

"Yes," Jacob said. "That is very true."

For a time they sat in silence, listening to the sound of the train as it beat past them, watching the wall of cars emerge from one horizon and disappear into another. It was a long train and Bertram wondered how many cars it might have, though he didn't bother to count them.

Jacob said, "There was something I'd been meaning to ask you about that machine you built."

"What about it?"

"I was wondering what you were really trying to prove with it?" Jacob said.

"I was trying to understand faith...to see how it works."

"I mean specifically what was the point?"

"Specifically? I'm not sure I know what you mean."

"I mean, what was it about faith that you were specifically trying to understand?"

"Everything," Bertram said.

"Weren't you really trying to measure the accuracy of my faith?"

"Well, yes. I guess I was."

"But the test was rigged," Jacob said, "because the only two choices you gave me were both wrong. And you knew they were both wrong."

"Yes, but that shouldn't have mattered, because God would have known the answer, and by your faith in Him, you would have known it too."

"And I did, didn't I? Because I predicted that the box was empty."

"Yes, but..."

"Shouldn't that prove something to you about the power of faith?"

"No, because you really didn't predict correctly."

"What do you mean? I said the box was empty, and it was. How could I have known that, if not by my faith in God?"

"Yes, you did eventually predict that the box was empty, that's true. But that wasn't your first choice. You first predicted that the ball would fall into the bucket. Remember? And that was wrong because the box was empty."

"So?"

"So I could have flipped the trapdoor open right there, and your prediction would have been proven wrong, only I didn't flip it. Instead, I stopped the test prematurely, which gave you a chance to change your mind. You probably saw something about me that made you suspicious—a look—something I said, the tone of my voice maybe."

"Okay, let's say that's true, but how could I have known specifically that the box was empty?"

"You know who I am. You know how I think. Remember that magic trick I showed you a long time ago, the one where I made a coin disappear by tapping it with a card?"

"No, not really."

"I was in Middle School. It was for the talent show."

"Sorry, no."

"The way it worked was that there was a magnet hidden inside the coin and an iron plate hidden inside the card. Remember?"

"I must have had other things on my mind. Sorry no."

"Maybe so, but your subconscious mind remembered it. The information was stored there, in your brain, and your conscious mind used it and made the connection. It was a logical guess. That's how you knew."

"It still doesn't explain why you decided to let me off the hook and give me another chance to guess the right answer. You said that you could have opened the trapdoor right there and proved me wrong if you had wanted to, only you didn't. Something must have stopped you from opening it."

"Yes, something did."

"What? What was it? What stopped you?"

Bertram smiled.

"Is something funny?"

"No. I was just thinking. You're very observant. Sometimes I think it's too bad that you're a preacher. You would have made an excellent scientist or a detective."

"Thank you, I think."

"You're welcome," Bertram said. "But to answer your question: What stopped me? Yes, I've asked myself that question too. I suppose it was morality that stopped me...or maybe guilt."

"Guilt? Morality? That's surprising," Jacob said, though he was clearly not surprised. "What were you feeling guilty about?"

"That thing I told you about Billy, about my grades in school."

"Why should that make you feel guilty?"

"Because I'd never intended to tell you about it. It was something I was going to keep secret forever, because I didn't want you to think badly of him."

"But the universe is amoral, Bertram. Why should it matter?"

"It doesn't matter…to the universe…because the universe is not alive. The universe doesn't have a conscience. But I do."

"Are you so sure? I mean about the universe. Are you so sure that it doesn't have a conscience?"

"Yes, from what I can see. The universe doesn't seem to care about what happens to us. It sends down rain to save us from dying of thirst one day, and then the next day tries to drown us with the very same 'miracle.' It gives us the earth to live on and to grow food on, and then tries to destroy what we build with earthquakes and mudslides. It doesn't care about morality because it doesn't even know that morality exists. It's just a machine. It creates and destroys without regard to beauty or to love or to what is good and to what is evil. It just acts, and we who do think, try to convince ourselves that there is some meaning behind the things that it does to us."

"Is that what you believe, Bertram?"

"It's what I see."

"What about your machine, the one you built, the one you made to test me? Do you think it's the same way too? That just because it isn't alive that it has no conscience. That it acts without regard to morality?"

"Of course. How could it be any different? It's just a machine."

"Ah, but that's where you're wrong Bertram. Your machine does have a conscience. It has a conscience because the person who built it and operates it has a conscience. The universe is no different. It too is a moral machine. It is a moral machine because the God, who created it and operates it, is moral. Just because we don't understand every decision that God makes on our behalf doesn't mean that He doesn't care about what happens to us. Everything that happens, happens for a reason, and everything that happens is either good or evil."

"That's what you believe by faith," Bertram said. "Not what you know by fact."

"You're always talking about facts and proof, Bertram, but can facts really lead us to the truth?" Jacob said. "That's the question you really should be asking yourself. Think about it, Bertram. How do we really ever prove anything to be true? By seeing it with our eyes? Is that really proof? I saw you operate your machine with my own eyes but it didn't help me to understand it. Our ancestors saw the Sun revolving around the Earth and they knew that that was true too, but as you pointed out to me before, they were wrong. 'Why were they wrong?' That's the question you should be asking yourself.

"They were wrong," Jacob said, "because they trusted what they thought they saw with their eyes, instead of relying on their faith in God to see what was really true. That's why faith is so important, Bertram, because without it we can only know what we think we see. That's what your experiment has really proven.

"And if we can't trust what we think we see with our own eyes," Jacob said, "then by what reference point do we live our lives, by what measuring stick do we judge our own actions? How can we try to be a good and moral people if we can't even see well enough to tell the difference between what is good and what is evil? If we can't trust the facts as we see them, then by what other realistic means do we have to see the truth except by our faith in God?"

Bertram smiled. It was a good point, but he had a better one. "So I guess that makes your car a moral machine as well?" Bertram said.

"It is if I'm driving it," Jacob said.

"But what about Mother Elizabeth? She's a moral person too, but she's not a very good driver."

"I assure you, Bertram, God knows how to drive...but then you don't believe in God, do you?"

"No, it's not that I don't believe in God. It's just that I don't know one way or the other if He's really out there, somewhere."

"And so you choose to believe in nothing?"

"I've found that believing in something, just because I'd like for it to be true, doesn't make it true."

"Everything is possible for him who believes," Jacob said.

"Believing makes it so? Sounds like a fairy tale."

"Believing doesn't make it true, Bertram. It is true, whether you believe it or not."

"To you."

"What about this then? You said that you could have opened the trapdoor and proven me wrong, but you didn't. Have you considered that it may have been God, speaking to you through the Holy Spirit who stopped you from opening the trapdoor to prove me wrong? That maybe it was God who reached out to your conscience with The Power of The Holy Spirit so that you might learn something about faith?"

"No," Bertram said, "but go on, explain it to me. I'm listening."

Jacob said, "In your eyes, even though I knew that the box was empty, you still feel, for some reason, that I didn't predict correctly."

"You didn't predict correctly. Not the first time."

"True, but you're missing the point."

"What?"

"You said that in order for you to understand how faith works that you were going to need to know what I was thinking and why I was thinking it. Isn't that so?"

"Yes."

"You said that's why you chose to study 'the faith that people have in gravity,' so as not to offend them or make them feel like you were ridiculing their religious beliefs."

"Yes."

"Well here's what I'm thinking. You've said that when I predicted wrong the first time that you could have opened the trapdoor right then, before I had a chance to change my mind, and proved me wrong."

"Yes."

"But here's the thing, Son. Even if you had, it still wouldn't have proven anything."

"Why?"

"Because in my mind—and that's what you said that you wanted to know, isn't it? What was in my mind?"

"Yes."

"Well in my mind, when I made that first wrong prediction, I didn't make it by my faith in God. I made it by my knowledge of the machine, and by my trust in you. That's where I went wrong. I didn't place my faith entirely in God. That's the reason I predicted incorrectly. But once I realized my mistake and I placed my faith completely in God, He revealed to me the truth; and that's when I knew that the box was empty!

"These are the facts as I see them, Son," Jacob said. "When I placed my faith in what I thought I understood about your machine and about gravity, I predicted incorrectly that the ball would fall into the bucket. But when I trusted in God alone for an answer, I predicted correctly that the box was empty. The meaning of those facts may seem inconclusive to you, but to me it is perfectly clear what they mean.

"I realize that you probably won't believe anything I've said," Jacob said, "but it's what I saw happen. I don't say this as your father, or as a preacher hoping to win your soul to Christ, or even as a friend. I say it strictly as a matter of record from the objective viewpoint of an expert on faith. That is what you asked me to do for you, isn't it?

"You said that you knew nothing of faith, that I was the expert, and if your machine was successful, that it would be up to me to tell you if the faith that it created was real or not. Well I'm telling you now Bertram. Your machine succeeded. It created faith in my mind. And it was real. It *is* real. I hope this information is useful to you in some way and that it helps you to find what you're looking for."

"Thank you," Bertram said. "I think it might."

"You're welcome, Son."

Suddenly a bright red caboose with darkened windows went racing past the front of the car and all was quiet again. The train was gone. The crossing arms were lifting. The warning lights stopped flashing. Jacob put the car into drive again, but just before he stepped on the gas pedal to cross the tracks, he said, "Remember, Son, I love you and I want you to know that you can call me anytime you need to, no matter the hour, no matter the circumstance. I'll be here to answer you."

"I know," Bertram said. "Thank you, Father. Thank you for everything."

"It was no trouble. We were very glad to have you, Son."

"I'll see you for Thanksgiving—maybe sooner—I was thinking about getting a job down there and buying a used car once I get settled," Bertram said.

"That would be nice. I'm sure you're Mother Elizabeth would like that."

"That's what I was thinking too—only don't tell her. I want it to be a surprise."

"I won't say a word, but make sure you call as soon as you get down there. You know how she worries."

"It'll be the first thing I do."

"Good. We'll keep you in our prayers."

"I appreciate that," Bertram said.

They made it to the bus depot on time and Bertram was in Florida before the day's end. He started classes the following week, but soon found that the people who ran The Florida School of Business Technology were not as patient with his questions as his Uncle Jacob had been, especially one of the deans at the school, the Dean of Philosophical Pursuits, Eliot Corbel.

CHAPTER 11

As Dean of Philosophical Pursuits, Eliot Corbel believed that human behavior was merely an extension of Natural Law. What some people consider immoral human behavior was, to Eliot, no more unethical than a lion eating a zebra on the African veldt. Just as a lion would do most anything to catch and to eat a zebra when it was hungry, so would a man do most anything to satisfy his hunger for money, providing the price was right.

So when the people of the world serviced Eliot's needs, and he gave them money in return for their services, whatever those services might be, he felt that he was simply following Natural Law by giving them what they most wanted in life, money. To deny them this opportunity to get from him the money that they desired would be to stymie the progression of Natural Law, and to Eliot this was an immoral act.

This Law, man's desire for wealth, Eliot had come to believe, was not only a Natural Law, but quite possibly a Universal Law that worked everywhere throughout the Cosmos—it was a law very similar to The Law of Gravity; Every Man had his Price. Every man would do Eliot's bidding, providing they were duly compensated for the full measure of their services.

But then Bertram Grey entered Eliot's world and everything for Eliot seemed to stop, for here was a man who did not want Eliot's money, though he was clearly in need of it. Here was a man who seemed to have no price. And that bothered Eliot. Why would someone not take something that was offered to him when he was clearly in need of it? It was incomprehensible, like a ball falling up instead of down! Something was wrong. Somehow The Natural Law of The Universe had gone awry. What had happened to The Law that Eliot believed he had once understood so clearly?

Who was this man, this Bertram Grey, who felt that he could quietly enter Eliot's world and disrupt it by disregarding The Rules of the Cosmos? Eliot remembered the day he first met Bertram Grey. Eliot was watching him from his office window. Bertram was wandering through the lobby on the second floor of the east wing of The Admin Building, following the signs on the walls, looking as if he wanted to ask someone a question.

Eliot rose from his desk and opened the door to his office and called out to him, "You look lost. May I help you? Who are you looking for?"

"I was trying to find Financial Aid."

"Maybe I can help you. What's your name?"

"Grey," Bertram said. "Bertram Grey."

"Oh yes, Mr. Bertram Grey. I reviewed you entrance exams. Very impressive. Please, come into my office, have a seat."

"Is this the Financial Aid Office?"

"No, but come in any way. I'm sure I can help you. My name is Eliot Corbel. I'm The Dean of Philosophical Pursuits."

"Oh, I guess I'm in the wrong place. They told me it was on the third floor."

"This is the second floor."

"No wonder I couldn't find it. Thanks."

"No problem. Hey, don't wander off so quickly. Since you're here, you may as well come into my office. I like to meet all the new students."

"I have an appointment with Financial Aid at 2:00."

"You still have a few minutes. There's no hurry. I think I may be able to help you with that. I have my fingers in all of the pies around here. If we run long, I can always reschedule you for another appointment. Who knows, after our meeting, you might not even need their help."

"Excuse me?"

"Please, come in." Eliot ushered Bertram into his office and offered him a chair. "Have a seat, Mr. Grey."

"I have an appointment with Financial Aid in ten minutes."

"Don't worry. There's plenty of time. If we run long, I'll give them a call and let them know you're on your way. Their office is just above mine. It only takes a few seconds to get up there."

"Oh, okay," Bertram said and reluctantly took a seat in the chair that Eliot offered him. Eliot returned to his desk and settled himself back down into a plush chair made of leather and oak. "Can I get you anything, Mr. Grey? A cup of coffee, a danish?"

"No sir, I don't drink coffee."

"A danish then?"

"I've already eaten breakfast, but thanks."

"Oh, okay. To each his own I guess. Bertram Grey?"

"Yes, that's Grey, with an 'E,' not an 'A.'"

"Okay, just let me type you in...and do a quick search here..." Eliot tapped on the computer keyboard on his desk. He scrolled through a series of screens until he apparently found what he wanted.

"Yes, here it is. Your entrance exams. I remember. With scores like this, what are you doing here, a bright young lad like yourself? No openings at Harvard or MIT?"

"No money," Bertram said. "That's why I was trying to find the Financial Aid Office."

"I'm sure I can help you with that."

"Oh, okay. What do we do?"

"I could write you a check right now for the full amount of your tuition."

"You could write me a check?"

"Yeah."

"Are you kidding? What's the catch?"

"No catch. I like you. You seem like an interesting guy. Come with me to France. This weekend. Have you ever been to France, Bertram? It's a beautiful country."

"I start class next week."

"So what? I'm a multibillionaire, Bertram. I can set it up so you won't ever have to work a day in your life. You'd like that, wouldn't you? Travel the world. See the sights."

"I appreciate the offer, sir. But I was hoping to get an education so I could get a job and send money home to my parents."

"A job? You don't need a job. All you need is money. I can give you that."

"In exchange for what?"

"For nothing. Because I like you. Come to Europe with me this weekend. Europe's a bore when you're alone."

Bertram was confused. "I..."

"This is the real world, Bertram. When you get older, you'll find out that there are no rules. We make up the rules. You can do whatever you want in this world providing you have the money to do it. I can give you the money. You, *we* could do with it whatever we wish."

"What's the catch?"

"No catch. You want an education. I want to take you under my wing and teach you about the world. How does that sound?"

"Teach me what?"

"About life, about how we make our own morality. I'm offering you the chance of a lifetime, Bertram, a chance to change the direction of your life. You can stay here, get a job, waste your time toiling away your life so that others can benefit from the spoils of your labor, or you can come with me to Europe, today. Now. You could be my Main Man. We could travel the world together. We could be buddies. You see Bertram that's the problem with being rich. Did you know that there's a problem with being rich?"

"Everyone has problems," Bertram said.

"The problem with being rich is that you find out that life is boring. That everything is all so meaningless, that nothing really matters. King Solomon figured that one out a long time ago. 'Everything is meaningless!' he said in

Ecclesiates. And he was right too. That's the great truth about life, Bertram. Nothing really matters!"

"The fall semester starts next week," Bertram said. "That matters to me."

"They'll be other fall semesters in other years. I'm offering you a free ticket to see the world, Bertram. Come see it with me."

Bertram still didn't know what to think.

"Tell you what. Just to let you know I'm serious. I'll write you a check for a thousand dollars and you can send it home to your parents. How's that sound?"

"Uh, thanks for the offer, but...I...think maybe I should go."

Bertram left Eliot sitting behind his solid oak desk, feeling very small.

Eliot Corbel did not like being made to feel small.

THE PARADOX AND THE STONE

Eliot met Bertram again while substituting a class on Business Planning and Economic Theory. Eliot generally knew very little about any of the subjects that he taught, so he usually spent the time dispensing his stale philosophies on life and told stories about his exploits in Europe and in Asia. He fancied himself a schooled philosopher, having graduated from one of those prestigious colleges with a high sounding name, and so he felt that his words commanded respect.

"Does anyone here know what a paradox is?" Eliot said to the class.

Bertram raised his hand.

"Yes, Bertram?"

Bertram said, "A paradox is like a contradiction."

"Yeah, like military intelligence," someone at the back of the room said.

"No," Eliot said. "That's only part of it. A paradox, a true paradox, is a statement that is seemingly contradictory at first, but in the end turns out to be true. Can anyone come up with an example of something like that?"

"The harder I study, the worse my grades get?" someone said.

"Maybe you're studying the wrong thing," another said.

"Yeah, I saw you studying that pitcher of beer last Saturday," said another. The class broke into laughter.

"Yes, that's a good one," Eliot said. "Any comments you'd like to offer, Bertram?"

"Yes," Bertram said. "The Atheist and the Christian are both alike."

"Yes," Eliot said with interest in his voice. "That is a paradoxical statement, but how is it true?"

"Both of them have faith. One has the faith to believe that there is a God, and the other has the faith to believe that there isn't one. If you can't prove that God exists, then how can you prove that He doesn't exist? So in either case, each chooses to believe what he believes by faith."

"Very good," Eliot said. "One of my favorite paradoxes about God is, 'Can God create a stone that is so heavy that He, Himself, cannot pick it up?'"

"How is that true?" Bertram said.

"It's true in that it dispels the absurd notion that an all-powerful God can exist, because if He can't make the stone, then He can't be all-powerful. But if He can make the stone, but then afterwards, can't pick it up, once again, He can't be all-powerful, you see?"

"No," Bertram said. "That's not what it proves at all."

"Oh?"

"No."

"Then tell me, Mr. Grey. What does it prove?"

"It proves that physical reality is the thing that is limited, not God."

"How so?"

Bertram said, "First, you have to look at the question itself because the question itself has implied limitations. Picking something up means that you and the object that you are about to pick up are both located on the surface of some central plane that is common to both. And what gives the stone its weight? What makes it heavy? The force of gravity. So the force of gravity is also implied. And what are the stone and the surface on which God is standing both made of?

"They're made out of the Universe," Bertram said, answering his own question. "So let's say that you are God, Mr. Corbel."

"I am in this classroom."

The classroom stirred with modest laughter.

Eliot calmed them. "Go on, Bertram," Eliot said. "Continue..."

"Okay," Bertram said, "So let's say you're God and you're floating in space and the Universe is all around you. And since we don't really know if the Universe is finite or infinite, for the purpose of this explanation we'll say that it is finite for now, but as you'll see in a minute, the proof works for both a finite and an infinite universe."

"Okay, I'll give you that for now," Eliot said.

Bertram said, "So there you are—God, floating in the middle of the Universe and you grab a handful of stuff and you pat it down into a ball. Then you grab some more stuff, and some more stuff, and you keep patting it down into the ball, making it bigger and bigger until you've used up all the matter in the Universe. When you're done, you climb up onto the ball. And now that's all that exists: God standing on a giant ball that's made out of all the stuff that's in the Universe.

"Now you're ready to test the paradox," Bertram said. "Can you make a stone that's so large that you can't lift it? So you grab a handful of stuff from the ball that you're standing on, and you make a stone. You lift it. Then you add some more stuff to the stone to make it bigger to see if you can lift that too.

"And of course you can because you're God and you're all powerful. But you want to be sure, so you keep adding more and more stuff to the stone on your back from the ball of stuff that you're standing on until you reach a point where the stone that you're lifting is just as large as the ball that you're standing on.

"Now you're no longer actually lifting a heavy stone, instead you are pushing two very large stones apart. But you still want to test the paradox completely, so you keep adding more and more stuff from the ball that you're standing on to the stone that's on your back. And what will eventually happen is that the ball that you're standing on will become so small that you can't see it, and the stone that you're lifting on your back will become so large that it will contain all of the matter in the Universe, except for one tiny little grain of sand, the tiny little grain of sand that you're still standing on.

"Now the question you have to ask yourself at this point is this: 'Are you actually lifting a very large stone on your back while standing on a ball of stuff that's the size of a grain of sand or are you just laying on your back with your feet up in the air looking a little silly?'

"And if the Universe is infinite," Bertram said, "the proof is still the same, because the stone that you're lifting on your back would be infinitely large and the ball of stuff that you're standing on would be infinitely small. So you see, it isn't God who is limited, because He *is* all-powerful. It is physical reality that is limited."

Eliot was silent for a moment, and then he began to slowly clap his hands together. "Bravo, Mr. Grey. You have defended your God very well. I'm impressed. So what kind of Christian are you? Surely not a Baptist? A Methodist perhaps?"

"I'm not any kind of a Christian, Mr. Corbel. I'm Agnostic," Bertram said.

"Bravo again, Mr. Grey," Eliot said.

THE NEGATIVE NEGATIVE

Eliot was at his desk when the phone rang. He picked it up.

"Hey, EL, it's Jim," the voice on the phone said. "Sorry, I'm not going to be able to make it in to school tomorrow. Say, when's this land deal going to come through? I didn't sign up for a J.O.B. I thought you said we were going to score quick. This gig is cramping my style."

"What's the class?"

"Business Math."

"Sure. I can take that one for you."

"Good. That annoying little twerp is in that class."

"Who?"

"Bertram-what's-his-name."

"Grey."

"Yeah that's the one. Mr. Know-it-all."

"Oh yes. Mr. Grey. Sure. It'll be my pleasure to take it for you," Eliot said.

"Good. That guy really gets under my skin. Oh, and if this land deal doesn't come through quick, you can count on taking over all my classes—permanently. See ya. Bye!" The connection went dead. Eliot keyed the phone off and placed it back into its charging cradle.

Bertram's second classroom interaction with Eliot Corbel had nothing to do with the existence of God or the topic of religion. In fact, it started out quite innocently as a discussion on credits and debits, which logically led to a discussion of positive and negative numbers, which then led to the question of: "Why does a negative number times a negative number equal a positive number?"

It was Eliot's answer to this question that caused the problem.

In answering the question, Eliot inadvertently said, "Oh, that's just something you have to take by faith. It's like a theorem in geometry. It's just true and you have to accept that it's true."

Of course Bertram's hand went up immediately.

"Yes, Mr. Grey?" Eliot said tiredly. "What is it?"

"That's not true. There is a perfectly logical explanation as to why a negative number times a negative number equals a positive number. And it has nothing to do with 'faith.'"

"Oh? And what is that, Mr. Grey?"

Bertram stood up from his desk. "May I?"

"By all means," Eliot said. He cleared his throat. "Attention class," he said. "Today's lesson will be given to you by Mr. Grey."

Bertram stood up and took a bow. "Good morning class," he said.

"Good morning Teacher," the class responded. There was some light-hearted jeering from the back of the room.

Eliot said, "Quiet now, I want to hear this."

The class settled.

"Continue Mr. Grey," Eliot said. "Class, please give Mr. Grey your undivided attention." Eliot was not being gracious or courteous in calling the class to order. He was simply prepping the class to be alert so that they could bear witness to how he was about to punch a hole in Bertram's explanation.

"Thank you, Mr. Corbel," Bertram said. Bertram took a black marker from the shelf at the bottom of the white board and drew a straight horizontal line across the board. "This is a road," Bertram said. "Let's call it Number Line Road."

Then Bertram took a green marker from the shelf and drew a car on the road with the headlights facing to the right. When he had finished that, he took a red marker and drew another car similar to the first only with the headlights facing to the left. He drew both cars close enough to each other so that the back bumpers of each car were touching.

Bertram said, "There are two cars on this road with their back bumpers chained together. Each car is trying to pull the other car in the opposite direction. It's like a game of tug-of-war. Whichever car goes the fastest is the direction that both cars will go. If the green car is going ten miles an hour, and the red car is going four miles an hour, then both cars will move in the green direction at six miles an hour, the green car dragging the red car. Okay?"

No one raised a hand to object.

Bertram said, "And let's call the green direction the positive direction and the red direction the negative direction. So if both cars are traveling at ten miles an hour, then the two forces will cancel each other out and the cars will stay in the same place. This is like saying positive ten plus negative ten equals zero. Now using this system, can anyone define for me the mathematical equation: $2 \times 3 = 6$?"

Again, no one raised a hand.

Bertram said, "It means that I take my foot, and I press it on the gas pedal of the green car, first once, which causes the green car to go three miles an hour faster. Then once again, without lifting my foot from the pedal, I press the pedal down further, which causes the green car to go three more miles an hour faster, for a total of six miles an hour faster than it was going before, so that in the end both cars will be traveling six miles an hour in the green (or positive) direction. The green car is dragging the red car six miles an hour in the green (or positive) direction."

The class seemed to understand this.

Bertram continued. He said, "Using this system, can anyone define: $3 \times 2 = 6$?"

Someone at the back of the room raised a hand.

"Yes?" Bertram said.

"Does it mean that you press the gas pedal on the green car three times and each time you press it down further, you go two miles an hour faster in the green direction?"

"Exactly," Bertram said. "So what about: $2 \times (-3) = (-6)$?"

"Does it mean that you press the gas pedal on the red car twice, and each time you go three miles an hour faster in the red direction?" someone said.

"Yes," Bertram said. "So what about: $(-2) \times 3 = (-6)$?"

No one answered.

"This one's a little tricky," Bertram said.

Finally someone said, "Does it mean that you lift your foot off the gas pedal in the green car two times and each time you do you go three miles an hour slower in the green direction so that the red car is able to drag the green car in the red direction six miles an hour?"

"Yes! That's it exactly. Both cars go in the red or negative direction. The green car isn't pulling with as much force as it used to, so the red car (the negative car) wins the tug-of-war and both cars move in the red or negative direction."

"Very good," Bertram said. "So what does: $(-2) \times (-3) = (+6)$ mean?"

The class was silent for a time until finally someone said, "Does it mean that you lift your foot off the gas pedal of the red car two times, and each time you do, you go three miles an hour slower in the red car?"

"Right!" Bertram said. "And what will happen? The green car will drag the red car in the green (or positive) direction at six miles an hour! So by the same token, $(-3) \times (-2) = (+6)$ means that you lift your foot off the gas pedal of the red car three times, and each time you do you go two miles an hour slower, which will give you the same result. You go six miles an hour slower in the red car, so the green car is able to drag the red car a total of six miles an hour in the green or positive direction.

"So you see," Bertram said, "All that a 'negative times a negative' really means is 'the removal of an opposing force.' And when you remove an opposing force, you will get more of the positive force."

Someone raised a hand.

"Yes?"

"Okay, I can see how that can work with forces, but what about something solid, like apples. How do you add a negative apple to a positive apple to get zero apples? There's no such thing as a negative apple."

"It's no different," Bertram said. "It's just that people get confused about what they're counting or how they're counting. They think that the number of things they count actually represents the number of things that exist, but they don't; they are two completely different things."

Eliot stood up from his desk. "Now that's ridiculous," he said. He had been seated at his desk with the remnants of his fast-food lunch still scattered before him.

Bertram pulled the plastic straw out of the lid on Eliot's cup of soda.

"Hey, I'm not done with that!"

"It's for instructional purposes," Bertram said. "You can have it back later."

"Forget it. It's yours."

Bertram said, "How many straws am I holding?"

"One," Eliot said.

"No," Bertram said. "There are actually two straws."

"I only see one."

"I know, but there are really two."

"Really?"

"Yes. There's an outside straw. See it? And there's an inside straw. See? The inside straw is slightly smaller than the outside straw and it's been crammed inside so that they're stuck together."

"Okay, if there are two straws, then pull them apart and show me."

"I can't. Like I said, they're stuck."

"Then there's only one," Eliot said.

"But what if I had two straws, one slightly smaller than the other and I could hold one in my left hand and one in my right hand? How many straws would I have?"

"I see where you're going with this. You're trying to get me to say that it's two straws, but it's not. It's still only one, because they're not the same size. Now if you had two straws that were exactly the same size, then there would be two, not two straws of different sizes."

"If I handed you a bag of apples and asked you to tell me how many apples there were inside, you'd count them and give me a number, and I'm pretty sure that all of the apples in the bag would be of different sizes."

"What's your point?"

"My point is that the physical object that you hold in your hand and the number that you assign to it in your mind are two completely different things. You could count just one apple in your mind or you could count ten positive apples and nine negative apples. Both systems are true. It's just a matter of convenience to say that there is just one apple because all of the other apples have cancelled each other out."

"Because there's just one apple."

"Okay, what about this," Bertram said. He reached over the top of Eliot's desk, and with one sweeping motion of his arm, slid the remains of Eliot's lunch into a nearby wastebasket.

"Hey! I wasn't done with that."

"It's for educational purposes," Bertram said.

"This better be good."

"Oh, it is," Bertram said. He took three markers from the white board and laid them on top of Eliot's desk. Bertram said, "The top of your desk represents the entire universe. It's everything that exists now or ever existed in the past or might exist in the future, black holes, worm holes, alternate realities—everything. Okay?"

"Sure, if you say so. But it still looks like the top of my desk to me." The class laughed softly, chuckling here and there, then quieted again.

"Well, trust me. It isn't. It's the entire universe."

"Okay, so what's your point?"

"The point is this. I want you to show me the mathematical operation: $3 - 1 = 2$."

"That's easy enough," Eliot said. "There are three markers on top of my desk and I take one away and..."

"No," Bertram said, interrupted him, "there are three markers in the entire universe and your desktop is the entire universe."

"Okay, there are three markers in the entire universe and I take one away. See? Now there are just two. Three minus one is two."

"Yes, but where did that marker go?"

"It's here in my hand."

"I said no alternate universes, remember? You can't remove the marker from the desktop because the desktop is the entire universe. There's no place else for it to go."

"Oh, okay. So now what?"

"So now put all three markers back in the universe."

"Like this?"

"Yes, now show me the mathematical equation: $1 + 2 = 3$."

"Oh, okay. Well, there's one over here by itself, and if I move it over here with these two, that equals three."

"Right. But from my point of view, just watching the movement of the markers, there was never any one plus two equals three. There were always just three markers that were moving around the universe. The math part of it exists only in our minds. We determine with our minds how many things there are. At one point you were saying that there was one marker over here and two markers over there, but there were only ever *three markers* moving around on your desktop, not one here and two there. Just three. So if you can take three markers and sometimes say it's one there and two here. Then what's the difference with looking at a single straw and saying that it's actually two straws: one on the outside and one on the inside? One over here and one over there."

"Because they're connected. These two markers aren't."

"No? I say that these two straws that I'm holding aren't connected either. There's a very thin layer of space separating them. It's a very small space, but it's there just the same, because as you know from your college physics class, solid matter is composed mostly of empty space. So now do you see what I'm saying?"

"Eh, no," Eliot said. "Class dismissed."

THE TERMITE AND THE DOUGHNUT

Eliot was beginning to check to make sure that Bertram was not in any of the classes that his buddies wanted him to substitute, and if he was, Eliot would decline; but sometimes even this tactic failed to save Eliot. On the last occasion that Eliot did substitute a class with Bertram Grey in it, the topic of free will came up.

Eliot believed in it; Bertram did not.

"There's no such thing as free will," Bertram said. "Human Behavior is a product of internal chemical reactions, set in place by preprogrammed instructions in our DNA which are set off by internal and external stimuli. We have no choice. We are basically organic computers with built-in pleasure centers that crave stimulation. Personally, I tend to ignore pleasure. I find it distracting."

"Why am I not surprised?"

"Fun is dangerous."

"Ah, but it is *you* who *chooses* not to have fun. You make that choice…that's free will!"

"No. It's not free will. It's just the way I'm made. I'm an aberration. It's natural selection. If two white rabbits mate they usually have white baby rabbits, but every now and then, through genetic mutation, they'll eventually wind up having a few babies that are not white.

"And if these rabbits are living in a place that's always covered with snow, chances are, the rabbits that are not white will get eaten by predators before they have a chance to mate and make little baby rabbits that aren't white either. So usually you'll only see white rabbits. But if for some reason the snow should suddenly melt, exposing the brown earth beneath it, then all of the white rabbits will get eaten first and now only the brown rabbits will survive to reproduce.

"That's the way it is with me," Bertram said. "I'm a white rabbit in a brown rabbit world. I'm preprogrammed to not really care too much about having fun. And if something were to happen that caused only the fun-loving-dancing people to die, maybe they all eat a bad batch of psychedelic mushrooms at one of their crazy parties or they all drown while they're having fun dancing on a cruise ship.

"Then only us quiet, not-so-interested-in-fun people will be left alive to have quiet prudent children who like to read. But that's okay, because every now and then, by chance and genetic mutation, a quiet, non-partying couple will give birth to a child who wants nothing else to do but to 'party hearty.'

"And later, who knows," Bertram said, "maybe all the boring quiet people who don't like to party may wind up dying in some kind of horrible library accident, leaving only the party-loving-people left alive, and then the whole process will start all over again."

"And that's the reason you claim to have no free will?" Eliot said.

"Yes. I'm like a termite."

"A termite?"

"Yes. Does the termite eat wood because it chooses to eat wood or does it eat wood because the bacteria in the termite's stomach want to eat wood? Is the termite really in charge of its own body, or is it merely a tool that the wood-digesting bacteria in the termite's stomach use to get the wood that they want? Which brings us to the question: 'Do I really have any desires of my own or are all my urges only a reflection of what the E-coli in my large intestine want?'"

"You can't be serious."

"I'm very serious. In fact, I've often wondered if world peace might not be achieved through the simultaneous evacuation of a World-Wide-Enema. Then we could implant every colon on the planet with the same E-coli to see what happens. Who knows, with everyone having the same desires, world peace might just be possible."

"That's ridiculous."

"Is it?" Bertram said, and he walked over to Eliot's desk, picked up a doughnut that Eliot was about to eat, and took a bite out of it.

"Hey, I was going to eat that!"

"Sorry. It wasn't me. It was my E-Coli," Bertram said.

Eliot said, "See me after class, Mister!"

CHAPTER 12

Bertram met with Eliot in the Dean's conference room after the class was over. When they were comfortably seated in opposing chairs, Eliot said to Bertram, "What do you want from me?"

Bertram said, "An education."

"An education in what?"

"Business Technology of course. That's why I'm here. To learn about Business Technology so that I can get a job and earn money."

"While you search for truth in your spare time?"

"We are all born to be philosophers. Isn't that what you always say?"

"Yeah, that's what I always say. So let me offer you a proposition."

"Why would you want to do that?"

"Because I like you."

"How is you're liking me going to help me to find the truth?"

"I'm rich. I can take you wherever you want to go. I can give you anything you think you might need to help you find the truth."

"I don't think that truth has anything to do with money."

"Now you're just being naive. Many of the great discoveries in science were made by men of leisure—men who had both the time and the means to investigate the great mysteries of life. That's what I'm offering you."

"Why?"

"Like I said, I like you. I want to see you succeed."

"Why?"

"You do ask a lot of questions, don't you? Come on. Don't be so suspicious. Believe it or not, I'm pretty smart too. I graduated from Harvard University. I know some things too. Why do you think I even started this stupid school? I don't need the money. The state practically gave me the land for free if I agreed to start a business on it."

"Why would they do that?" Bertram said.

"To employ people; to increase the city's tax base; to stimulate the economy; it's all about growth! In a few years after the school folds, I'll shut it down, sell the land to a developer who will pay me millions for it, and I only put in a couple hundred thousand. Even better, I can write the whole venture off as a loss and pay virtually no taxes on the profits. Pretty smart, eh?"

"Why would you do something like that if you don't really need the money?"

"Haven't you been listening? I'm bored! Life is boring!"

"It sounds immoral," Bertram said.

"What's your problem? I didn't kill anybody or steal anything. I didn't even break any laws—oh I get it—if it doesn't go according to your set of high moral values, then it's immoral because you're better than everyone else is. That's it, isn't it?"

"No. I'm not better than everyone else."

"That's right, you're not! You just *think* you are!"

"No I don't. I'm just like everyone else."

"Oh now that's a lie!"

Bertram shifted uneasily, "So what do you want from me?"

"What if I told you that I had definitive proof as to the existence of God?"

"I wouldn't believe you."

"Of course not, because that's just the kind of arrogant jackass you are! You expect everyone else to listen to you when you start going on about truth and morality and negative numbers. You expect everyone else in the world to listen to you, but you don't give a flip about what anyone else has to say."

"What do you have to say?"

"I'm saying that I have proof about the existence of God."

"Okay. I'm interested. Tell me. I'm listening."

"No, not here. You'd only give it the brush off. What I have to show you can't be told. It has to be seen."

"So show me."

"You serious?"

"Yes. Show me. I want to see what you've discovered."

"It's not here. We'll have to fly there."

"Where to? *France*?" Bertram said sarcastically.

"No, jackass. It's in South America."

"South America?"

"Yeah. Believe it or not, sometimes you have to go digging for the truth. It's not out in the open. It's buried deep. But you won't come with me. I know your type. You won't go. You already have all the answers. You already have everything figured out."

"No I don't."

"Then come with me."

Bertram wasn't sure how to respond.

"You see. That's your problem," Eliot said. "You don't really want to know the truth. That would spoil your game. You don't really care about 'The

Truth.' If somebody came up to you with the real truth, you wouldn't give him the time of day. All this talk of truth and morality—it's just a game with you. Something you can use to lord over all the ignorant masses to make yourself look superior."

"That's not true. I'm just not interested in the things that most people are. Like I said, I'm a white rabbit in a brown rabbit world. I'm just not interested in temporal things or temporal pleasures. They don't last. I'm searching for The Eternal."

"The Eternal? Ha! Now that's the first true thing that you've said about yourself. You aren't interested in temporal things! But you seem to forget Mr. Grey, people are temporal things…they don't last!"

"I'm not talking about people."

"That's right, you never talk about people. People aren't important to you, except to have as an audience to belittle anyone who disagrees with you!"

"That's not true."

"Then prove it. Come with me to South America. Let me show you what I've discovered about God!"

"Okay," Bertram said without hesitation. "I'll go with you then. Show me what you know about God. I'll listen."

So Bertram Grey went with Eliot Corbel to the jungles of South America. He was with Eliot for two months, searching the rain forests of South America for God. And to Bertram's great surprise, Eliot did keep his promise, for Bertram did find God.

CHAPTER 13

When Bertram Grey returned home from South America, he found that many things had changed in the quiet town of Pietyville, South Carolina. Temple Creek Baptist Church and Christian Youth Academy had burned down. Bertram's Aunt Elizabeth had been killed when the crossing arm at the railroad track near the bus depot had failed to operate and she didn't see the train that was crossing the intersection. Bertram's Uncle Jacob had suffered a stroke two days after the accident and was laying in a coma in a bed at Pietyville Memorial Hospital and Christian Refuge for the Aged.

As tragic as all of these events may have appeared to most people, Bertram knew that they were not tragic at all. For he knew that his Aunt Elizabeth was now in Heaven, a member of a Chorus of Angels singing eternal praises to God. He knew that Temple Creek Baptist Church and Christian Youth Academy would, one day, rise from the ashes to be grander and more beautiful than it had been before. He also knew that his Uncle Jacob would soon awaken from his coma. Bertram knew these things because God had revealed them to him by The Power of The Holy Spirit.

A young female nurse in green surgical coveralls led Bertram down a series of hallways to a door labeled 214 West. "He's in here," she said quietly, stopping at the door before opening it. "We took him off the ventilator two days ago. He's been doing very well. He's stable now. All of his vitals are good."

"Good," Bertram said. "Is he still in a coma?"

"Yes," she said and opened the door for him to enter.

"Thank you," Bertram said, stopping at the threshold to look into the room. His Uncle Jacob lay in a hospital bed, on his back, eyes closed, breathing softly. His mouth was slightly opened. His wrists were strapped to the bed railings.

His facial features appeared skeletal, the eye sockets darkened and hollow. His hair was oily and matted. His lower face was stubbled with beard. He looked much older than Bertram remembered him, but perhaps it was a trick of the lighting, the shadows falling on his face in strange patterns. Had it really been just two months since Bertram had left Pietyville for South America?

Somehow it seemed much longer.

The nurse said, "He rested well last night. We still have his hands restrained to keep him from pulling out his IV tubing."

"Has he said anything?"

"No. Not that I've heard. And there's nothing in his chart that says anything about him speaking."

"Oh, okay. Thanks."

"I have to make my rounds now," the nurse said, "but if you have any questions or need anything, there's a call button on the console on the bed. It's the red button there, on the railing. Someone at the front desk will answer."

"Okay," Bertram said, quietly. "Thank you."

"You're welcome," she said and left the room.

When Bertram was certain that she was gone, he dragged a wooden stool over to the bedside and sat there for a time, watching his uncle in silence. He leaned in close to Jacob's ear and said, "Hello Father. I've come back, like I said I would." Then standing, but not taking his eyes from his uncle's sleeping form on the bed, Bertram reached into the collar of his shirt and pulled at a braided silver chain that he wore around his neck.

The chain pulled out of Bertram's collar to reveal a smooth silver locket attached to the end of it. Bertram held the locket in the open palm of his right hand. With the thumb of the same hand he pressed a raised button along the curved edge with his thumbnail. The lid on the locket sprung open to reveal a bit of pastel blue and green within.

Bertram touched this patch of color with the thumb of his right hand and reached out to Jacob with his left hand, palm-side down, placing it on Jacob's forehead. Bertram closed his eyes and bowed his head as if in silent prayer. His lips moved indistinctly, forming words that had no sound, his eyelids closed and relaxed.

He remained in this posture for about a minute, when suddenly his closed eyelids squeezed tight and his jaw line hardened, his facial expression contorted, as if reacting to a sudden spasm of pain. When this had passed, he opened his eyes and turned his head so he could see the stool behind him. Using the guardrail on the bed for support, he lowered himself close to the stool, dropping heavily onto the padded seat at the last moment, as if exhausted by some unseen ordeal against which he had struggled.

Jacob moaned softy and stirred in his sleep.

Once seated on the stool again, recovering his strength, Bertram pinched the locket together until he felt the lid snap into place. He placed the locket back into the collar of his shirt where it hung again from his neck by the braided sliver chain.

Jacob's eyelids stirred and opened suddenly.

"Where am I?" he said, more to himself than to Bertram.

Bertram said, "You're in the hospital. They say you had a stroke."

Jacob sat up, a little too quickly, and faltered. Bertram supported him and helped ease him back down. "Not so fast. You've been in a coma for about a week."

"Elizabeth..."

"Yes, I know," Bertram said. "Be at peace. She's in Heaven now. She's happy. I know. God told me."

"God told you?"

"Yes."

"What...?"

"I found God."

"You found God?"

"Yes."

"That's nice," Jacob said and he drifted back to sleep.

THE DEMON CALLED LEGION

While traveling in the territory of Gerasenes, Jesus removes the demon called Legion from a possessed man. After removing this demon, Jesus does not cast it into The Abyss. Instead, Jesus casts it into a herd of swine that is feeding on a hillside. Afterwards, the possessed herd rushes into a nearby lake and all the swine are drowned. Why does Jesus do this? What is the purpose of this action? Does it help to shed light on a Fundamental Supernatural Law?

—Commentary from The Gospel According to Bertram,
Book Two, Chapter Two—

Jacob recovered quickly after waking from the coma. Three days later, Bertram took him home. They were in the den, Jacob seated at his desk, Bertram standing near the fireplace, watching him.

"How long was I out, you said?" Jacob said.

"About a week."

"A week?"

"You went in on the eighth, they said. Today is—what—the nineteenth?"

"I guess so?"

"Yeah, so about a week. Would you like another cup of coffee?" Bertram said.

"Sure."

Bertram was about to set the cup in front of Jacob, when a sudden tremor shook Bertram's hand, spilling coffee onto the desktop.

"Are you okay?" Jacob said.

Bertram stretched out the fingers of his right hand, closed them into a fist, stretched them out again. "Yeah, I'm okay," he said.

"You sure?"

"I'm sure."

"You don't look so sure."

"No. I am. I was just wondering...about you. How do you feel about traveling?"

"Traveling? Where?"

"To Nevada."

"Nevada?"

"Yes, I need to go to Wheeler Peak."

"Wheeler Peak?"

"It's a mountain. There's going to be an eclipse of the sun next month. It will be total over Wheeler Peak."

"Yes, I remember hearing about it before I had the stroke."

"I have to go there."

"Why?"

"God told me to go there."

"God told you?"

"Or maybe it's The Holy Spirit, or both. I'm not really sure."

"Put your hand out again, Son," Jacob said. Bertram held out his right hand, fingers stretched out. The hand trembled steadily.

"Your hand. What's wrong with it?"

"Nothing. I'm fine."

"You don't look fine to me."

"Believe me. I'm fine. How are you?"

"Fair. Considering I just had a stroke."

"It wasn't a stroke," Bertram said. "You were possessed by a demon. I removed it. That's why you came out of the coma. That's why you recovered so quickly."

"A demon?"

"Yes, a demon. You still believe in them, don't you?"

"Yes, but it didn't feel like a demon. It felt more like a stroke."

"Of course. That's what it wants you to believe. If it had made you aware of its presence, it knows that you would believe everything that I'm about to tell you and help me. It doesn't want that. It wants you to think that I'm crazy and call the police so that they can come and lock me up. That's what it's counting on. Your disbelief, your lack of faith."

"I don't think I'm following you, Son."

"It's all in here," Bertram said. "I've been tracking it." Bertram opened up a canvas bag and scattered the contents across Jacob's desk, newspaper clippings, photographs, spiral binders, folders stuffed with ragged looking papers, a large silver crucifix, a thick leather bound Bible filled with numerous bookmarks.

"Here," Bertram said. "This is where it begins." Bertram picked up The Bible and showed it to Jacob. Jacob noticed that the spine had been cut down the middle, from top to bottom and a strip of white inserted between the two halves. "I added my own book," Bertram said. "It's called *The Gospel According to Bertram*. Don't worry; I got permission first. I'll read to you from Chapter One."

Jacob was alarmed, but he tried not to show it.

Bertram opened the Bible and began to read from it. He said, "And behold, Bertram Grey, a poor student of faith, followed Eliot Corbel, an evil man, into the rainforests of South America in search of God. They journeyed deep within the jungle-land to a Place of Rains and Mists, where a tribe of dark-skinned peoples worshipped The Mighty Tree. The Sacred Memories tell us, when The God of the Air first created All Things, there was a Great War in the Heavens.

"The God of the Air defeated the Demons of the Mists and cast them out of the Heavens and into The Mighty Tree. But The God of the Air became entangled and was pulled down with them also into The Tree, to remain trapped with them until The Day when The Sun goes Dark and All Things End.

"Then Eliot Corbel, the evil man, said to Bertram Grey, 'This is the truth that I will show you in the rain forests of South America, that there is no God! For if there was a God, He would stop me. But He will not stop me because He does not exist! I will wash away the land with my Machines and pull up the trees and mix together with them mercury to extract the gold and lay waste to every good thing for my own profit!'

"Bertram Grey said to the evil man, 'There may or may not be a God, but if He won't stop you, I will!' And Bertram Grey threw himself at the evil man, Eliot Corbel, to keep him from destroying Creation, but the evil man cast sticks of dynamite at Bertram Grey and the ground ripped apart beneath his feet as if torn to pieces by Unseen Hands made of Thunder and Flame.

"Water gushed forth from The Great Machines, as another stick of dynamite flew from the Demon Hand of Eliot Corbel. The ground ripped open again and The Mighty Tree fell, trapping Bertram Grey beneath it.

"The Flood waters rose, taking with it the air.

"Bertram Grey choked and could not breathe.

"For a measure of time that had no number all was dark.

"The Earth groaned and the waters of The Great Flood receded. And Bertram Grey was held up, alive within the branches of The Mighty Tree. The End Times had come for The Mighty Tree was dead. And the God of the Air and the demons held therein were released into the world.

"The demons fled. But The God of the Air did not. He took bodily possession of the man called Bertram Grey and commissioned him to find the demons and to stop them from their Evil Designs," Bertram closed The Bible and he looked to Jacob and he said, "The Word of God."

Jacob was frightened. He said, "Son? Are you okay? What's happened to you? What are you talking about? I don't understand."

"I know God exists!" Bertram said. "That's what this is all about. I know because He's here, inside my head. I can hear His Voice. It's God, The One True God, The God of Abraham."

"Son, you're scaring me."

"I know God exists, Father. He's finally talking to me out loud just like He did with Moses and Saint Paul!"

"Then what were you talking about before? This god of the air and demons in the trees? What was that all about?"

"The God of the Air and The God of Abraham. It's the same God!"

"How do you know?"

"If God were to descend from the Heavens this very day, as a Steel Ball Bearing exactly one mile across so that all would see Him exactly the same, everyone would still see Him differently. That's the way it is. We are all separate in our perception of reality. It is impossible for two separate people to ever see God in exactly the same way! And just because two different people see the same God differently doesn't mean that there are two different gods. It's still just The One God. Do you see?"

"Who told you this?"

"God did."

"God spoke to you?"

"Yes. He speaks to me. It's like you always told me, Father. God does speak out loud, sometimes. But only to special people, people like Moses and Saint Paul. And now He's finally speaking to me, Father. With His own Voice! I can hear him!"

"What does His voice sound like?"

"Interestingly enough, it sounds a lot like my own voice," Bertram said. "But don't you see how that makes perfect sense? He's using this body—the brain, the vocal cords, the ears of this body, as a communication device to talk to me, like a cell phone, or a radio receiver. So of course He's going to sound like me!"

"What's He saying to you? What does He want?"

"He wants me to find the demons that escaped when Eliot Corbel destroyed The Mighty Tree. He wants me to find them and to capture them!"

"How?"

"With this," Bertram said, reaching into the collar of his shirt with the fingers of his right hand to pull at the chain that held the silver locket. Bertram held the locket in the open palm of his hand to show his uncle.

"What is it?"

"It's an amulet—a locket," Bertram said. "See? It opens." Bertram pressed the side of the locket with his thumbnail and the lid opened up. Jacob looked inside. "What's in it?"

"It's a patch of blue-green lichen. When I catch one, I put it in here to hold it to keep it from escaping." Bertram saw confusion in his uncle's eyes. "Remember the demon called Legion?" Bertram said.

"Yes."

"Jesus put Legion into a herd of pigs."
"Yes?"
"Would you be more convinced if I had a pig on a leash and I told you that I was going around catching demons and putting them inside of a pig?"

Jacob didn't say anything. He didn't know what to say. Finally he said, "No. I don't think so." Jacob looked down at one of Bertram's files. The contents had spilled out onto the desktop. It was a collection of newspaper articles. The headlines read:

CONGRESSMAN LEAPS TO HIS DEATH
WILDERNESS RECLAMATION ACT PASSES SENATE
CONDOS? SEQUOIA NATIONAL PARK, HOUSE APPROVES
CEO FOUND DEAD IN HOTEL ROOM
TOTAL ECLIPSE OVER WHEELER PEAK
RITUAL BATHTUB DROWNINGS INVESTIGATED
SENATOR FOUND DEAD IN DC PARKING LOT
LOBBYIST DIES IN FIERY CRASH

There were others.
"Bertram," Jacob's voice cracked. "You didn't kill these people, did you? Tell me you didn't...kill...them. Son...Speak to me."
"No Father, I didn't kill them. The demons did."
"Son. You're scaring me."
"You should be afraid Father, but not of me."

HELL IS GREEN AND THERE IS NO BRIMSTONE

Bertram said, "They've been waiting for over four thousand years for this day."
"Who's been waiting?" Jacob said.
"Next month is the Sixth Day of the Sixth Month of the Sixth Year of the Last Millennium. They weren't trying to stop Corbel, only delay him."
"I'm not sure, I..."
"The solar eclipse in Nevada; Corbel and his condominium resort in Sequoia National Park; Senator Jenken's death in DC; Congressman Forbes's suicide in the hotel room. It's a pattern. Look," Bertram arranged the newspaper clippings on Jacob's desk in chronological order. "It all makes sense now. The demons weren't trying to stop Corbel from building a condominium resort in Sequoia National Park...only delay him. They couldn't allow him to start building before the sixth of June."

Jacob was still trying to make some sense out of what Bertram was saying.

Bertram said, "Over four thousand years ago, God cast Satan and his angels from the heavens. 'Hurled them to the Earth,' The Bible says. But where on Earth did He hurl them?"

"He hurled them into Hell," Jacob said.

"Then Hell must be somewhere on Earth?"

"The Bible doesn't say."

"That's right. It doesn't say. It doesn't say because we were never supposed to know where it was. We couldn't be trusted with the truth. The truth was too dangerous."

"What truth?"

Bertram said, "It's the Eternal Dilemma. The Problem that has plagued both man and God since the beginning of time: What to do with those members of society who refuse to live within the boundaries of the law? We as men have two options: imprisonment or death. But what do you do when the criminal is not a man? What do you do when the criminal is an immortal entity—one that can neither be killed nor held captive in a prison cell made of mere bricks and steel?"

"That's what Hell is for."

"Yes, I agree. But what exactly is Hell? No one really seems to know. Even we as Christians can't seem to agree on a single answer. There's that fire and brimstone version of Hell, but if a demon can pass through a steel wall as easily as we can pass though air, then how can a lake of mere fire and brimstone hold it?"

"It's a Divine Fire."

"Maybe. Or maybe it's not that at all."

"It's a supernatural force. Demons are, after all, supernatural beings. It only makes sense that it would require a supernatural force to restrain them."

"But aren't we too, as people of God, supernatural beings? Aren't our souls immortal entities? Aren't we just one step away from the angels? Yet here we are, trapped within the limitations of our own physical bodies, as Legion was trapped when Jesus placed him inside a herd of pigs."

"Yes. We talked about that I remember."

"But pigs make bad prisons. Demons are elusive and cunning. To imprison a demon effectively you need something a little less mobile than a pig. A pig can be made to drown itself in a lake, or to jump off a cliff, or to starve itself to death if you don't force-feed it. And once it's dead the demon that was trapped inside of it is free again. No, a pig is too unstable a thing to hold a demon."

Bertram said, "The perfect prison for a demon would have to be something living that can't move at all; something that can thrive on a diet of water, air, and sunlight so you don't have to worry about it starving itself to death. What is needed is something with a very long life-span, so you don't have to keep swapping the demon over into to a new host every time the old host dies of old age."

"Sounds like you're describing a tree."

"Yes, but not just any kind of tree. Something large enough to hold 'the third of all the angels' cast down from Heaven, something with a life-span long enough to make sure that they stay there for a very long time."

"A sequoia tree?"

"Thirty-nine sequoia trees, to be exact. Thirty-nine giant sequoia trees, growing in a secluded grove in a southwest region of Sequoia National Park."

"So what are you saying, Bertram? That Sequoia National Park is the Biblical Hell?"

"No, not all of it. Just the one grove of the thirty-nine trees."

"And this man—what was his name?"

"Corbel."

"And this man, Corbel, was going to chop them down to build resort condominiums?"

"Just another good reason not to chop down very old trees. It isn't always about conservation and ecology."

"What about the Lake of Fire?"

"It never existed."

"Then the Bible's a fake and God's a liar?"

"What else could He do, Father? Tell us the truth?"

"Think about it, Bertram. None of this makes any sense. If God was going to put demons into trees, he would have warned us so that people like Corbel would have picked another place to build his condos."

"Warned us, Father, how? By placing the trees in a prominent place—say, in the middle of a garden, perhaps—and warn us—how? By telling us not to chop them down, because if we did, then 'we would surely die?' Correct me if I'm wrong, Father, but didn't He already try that once with a tree of another kind? And we all know how that turned out, don't we?"

"But if what you're saying is true, Son, then why didn't He choose some place more remote than Sequoia National Park?"

"Four thousand years ago, it was the most remote place in the world...across the span of a vast uncertain ocean, on the far side of a continent that was not yet known even to exist."

"Okay, okay, but if Sequoia National Park is the Biblical Hell, like you say it is, isn't that in California?"

"Yes it is."

"Then why do you want to go to Nevada?"

"What good is an army without its Commander-in-Chief?"

Jacob puzzled over Bertram's reply. He hadn't expected so quick a response to his objection. Jacob thought he had found a contradiction in Bertram's story, something that he might have been able to use to shake Bertram's mind loose from the delusion that had taken hold of it.

Bertram said, "It's never wise to imprison the leader of an army with his own troops. You keep him isolated, exiled from the others, alone..."

Jacob listened, hoping for another opportunity to awaken Bertram's mind from the insanity that clouded it.

Bertram said, "On the Northeast face of Wheeler Peak stands that solitary prison cell, a bristle cone pine tree that has stood for over four thousand years, but after June Sixth, it will stand no more."

"Why? What are you talking about?"

"An occult group, The Detested Ones, they plan to destroy the tree at the apex of the solar eclipse, on June sixth, to release their Leader. Once he has been released into the world again, he will use whatever means necessary to destroy all of Sequoia National Park to free his army of demons and bring about Armageddon!"

"Their Leader? You mean Satan?"

"You still believe in him, don't you?"

"Yes, yes, of course, but that he lives in a tree, like an elf? No."

"God appeared to Moses as a bush."

"I really don't think it's the same thing."

"Why not?"

Jacob couldn't think of a good answer, so he asked a question. "What about this Mighty Tree you were talking about, the one in South America? I thought The God of the Air dragged all of the demons down with him and trapped them there?"

"That was The Last Battle in a long War. Most of the demons, a third of them, were hurled into Sequoia National Park when The War first started. Sometimes God has to improvise."

"What does that mean? God is All Powerful. He can do anything He wants. Nothing can stop Him."

"Yes, that is true, Father. God is All Powerful, but physical reality has its limitations. Nothing can travel faster than the speed of light. No two objects can occupy the same place at the same time. God has to work within the limitations of physical reality to keep Creation from being torn apart. A surgeon must cut into a patient in order to save his life, but he must be careful about what he is cutting and where he is cutting, or he will kill the person that he is trying to save. It's the same way with Creation, and God is The Surgeon."

"Okay, okay, but if these demons really are trapped inside sequoia trees, then why were they trying to *stop* Corbel from building his condominiums? It seems to me that they would want to try to help him."

"What good is an army without a leader? Satan had to be released first. They had to stop Corbel because The Release has to be timed with the apex of the solar eclipse. It marks the time of God's greatest vulnerability. Didn't a celestial event mark the birthplace of Christ the King?"

Jacob said, "I know all of this must seem to make sense to you, Bertram, but have you considered another possibility? I know I have always encouraged you to think less and to pray more. But maybe now is the time to ask God to help you to *think* better. Think Bertram. Think. Remember. The Mad Hatter. *Alice in Wonderland*. How did the Mad Hatter get his name?"

Bertram thought about this and he remembered.

He knew exactly how the Mad Hatter got his name.

THE MAD HATTER AND THE HOLY GHOST

During the 19th Century, mercury was used in the making of hats to stiffen the brims. The workers who made these hats, the hatters, would often suffer from mercury poisoning which caused neurological damage to the brain, making the hatters appear confused or disturbed, hence the phrase, "mad as a hatter."

Jacob said, "I have an idea. Remember when you tested me with your machine to see how faith worked? You said that I was the expert and you wanted me to tell you if the faith that it created was real or not?"

"Yes."

"Why not let this spirit, or whatever it is, leave your body and come into my body? That way I can see if..."

"If it's real or not?"

"No. So I can see if it is of God or if it is of the Devil."

"That won't work."

"Why not?"

"Once a demon or any other spirit-form enters a living physical body, it becomes trapped there. The spirit-force and the life force of the host fuse together and can't be separated until the body dies and the electrical patterns of the physical body dissipate. Then the spirit-form can untangle itself from the host body and move on to inhabit another host."

"Yes, but this spirit that's in you...it seems to have the power to remove demons from people without having to kill them. It removed the demon inside of me without having to kill me. Why can't it use this same power on itself to leave your body and enter into me so that I can study its nature."

"It doesn't work that way," Bertram said. "Removing a demon from a living host requires a kind of Spiritual Leverage."

"Leverage?"

"Yes, you and I weigh pretty much the same, yes?"

"I suppose."

"And even if you weighed a little more than I did, I could still take hold of your body, pick it up, and place it up onto a step or a raised platform, if it's not too much higher than where I'm standing. But no matter how hard I try, even if I weigh less than you do, I still can't grab hold of my own body and pick it up and place it up onto the same platform. Do you see?"

"I'm not sure..."

"Removing a demon from a host is very similar. When the spirit entity that's inside of me uses me to remove a demon from a host, it is in a way, picking up the demon and placing it up onto a higher step. And in the same way that I can't pick up my own body, the spirit being inside of me can't remove itself from this body and go into you."

"I see."

"But that doesn't mean that your proposition is not without merit. There are two ways that it can be done. (1) Another spirit-form of equal or greater power, could pick it up out of me and place it into you, or (2) you could kill me or I could kill myself, and once my life force dissipates, it could untangle itself from my physical body and go into you."

"I see."

Bertram said, "Don't worry, Father. I'm not crazy. I'm not asking you to kill me, and I'm not suggesting that I should kill myself. I'm just giving you the facts. You asked the question. That's the answer, inconvenient as it may be. You said you wanted me to think. Well here's what I think.

"Maybe you're right," Bertram said. "Maybe I do have elevated mercury levels in my blood stream. But maybe that's what my body needed to fix the part of my brain that allows me to know that God exists. Scientists say that our brains are either "hard-wired" for faith or not. You either know that God exists or you don't know that God exists. It's not a choice. You are born that way.

"I used to be an unbeliever. I was born that way. But now I'm not. Now I know that God exists. Maybe the mercury in my bloodstream has rewired my brain somehow to let me know that God exists. And now that I do know, I'm not willing to give that up for anything. Even if I agreed to go with you to see a doctor and he told me that there was mercury in my blood and that it was causing me to know that God exists. I certainly wouldn't let him cure me!"

"I understand, Son."

Bertram said, "My whole life has been a journey towards God. You were there guiding me and helping me when I needed you most, encouraging me, without appearing judgmental or sarcastic. You let me ask my questions and do my little tests on you to try to figure out the answers on my own. And now I believe, Father! Now I *know* that everything you tried to tell me is true!

"God is real. Jesus is His Son," Bertram said. "There is a Heaven. There is a Hell. God was a Burning Bush. God was a Cloud. God was a Pillar of Fire. There was a Tree of Life. There was a Tree of Knowledge. So maybe there are other kinds of trees too, trees that God didn't tell us about. Creation is a Great Mystery. Does anyone really understand it all? No. I don't think so. But the one thing that I do know is that where there is God, there is love and there is understanding. And with God's Love and with God's understanding all things *are* possible. We can't fail."

"That is true, Son," Jacob said. "Very true. With God's love, all things *are* possible. You are right. We can't fail. We won't fail. Tell me, Son. What's our next step? Where do we go from here? What must we do?"

"Wheeler Peak," Bertram said. "We have to stop the Detested Ones before they release Satan. But first I'll have to test the tree, to make sure that it's still alive and that Satan is still in it."

"Yes," Jacob said, "Then that is what we must do. You'll test and I'll guide…"

THE EPILOUGE

CHAPTER 1

Perhaps you are wondering what became of Bertram and his uncle? Did they make it to Nevada before the solar eclipse on the sixth of June? Were they able to stop The Detested Ones from releasing Satan from the four-thousand-year-old bristle cone pine tree on Wheeler Peak? Were the demons even real? And hey, is the story over? It did just say THE EPILOUGE on the previous page.

Well, yes.

Those are all very legitimate questions.

But the answer is this: None of those things really matter, because that's not the point of the story. Then what is the point of the story? You may wonder. And therein lies the problem. My point may not necessarily be the true point of the story.

I say this because, having been on this planet for more than half a century, I've noticed a few things about life. One thing I've noticed about life is that the people who write the books or paint the pictures or make the movies, often times, don't really understand the true meaning behind the work that they produce.

And sometimes it takes someone else, someone who is watching the painter or the writer or the artist, to determine the work's true meaning. So I won't even bother to tell you what I think about it, only why I thought to write it. And that's easy, because that's an entirely different story. And it all started at...

THE TOP OF A GUMBALL TREE

I was in the second grade at Millington Elementary School in Atoka, Tennessee. My father was in the Navy so we moved around a lot. I was born in Agana, Guam, and by the time I made it to the second grade I had gone to three different elementary schools.

My older sister, Vilita, and I had climbed to the top of a gumball tree that grew in our front yard close to the road. My father used to park his car beneath it. I don't remember exactly how tall the tree was, but I do remember that it was taller than the roof of our house, so it was pretty tall—tall enough to break your neck if you fell out of it. And we probably shouldn't have been up there to begin with, but kids will be kids and we were up there anyway.

We had been up in that tree for at least one or two minutes, so quite naturally, we were already bored. So I looked at my sister and my sister looked at me, and one of us said, "Let's race down. First one wins!"

"Ready, set, go!"

And we were off!

I was pretty much winning, most of the way down, and then I missed a branch. And then I was really winning, because I was falling. And I kept falling. I seemed to fall forever. I remember seeing bits of branches and green leaves flashing out in front of me, a patch of blue above, the white gravel below, everything was just beyond my reach. My arms and legs were flailing out, searching for something to grab. It was all very automatic. I wasn't really thinking to do anything. My body was just reacting.

And then suddenly, I stopped falling.

I was impossibly suspended in mid-air.

It took me a few seconds to realize what had happened.

A lower branch had caught me lengthwise, just before I was about to hit the ground. I hung there for a few seconds, dazed, still not thinking. Just hanging there. My right arm and my right leg dangling off one side of the branch, and my left arm and my left leg dangling off the other side of the branch. When I finally came to my senses, and I shook myself and I realized that nothing was broken, I looked down below and I saw my sister standing on the ground looking up at me. She was smiling.

She said, "I win!"

A few days later or a few weeks later (I'm not really sure which) I woke up in the middle of the night with a terrible headache. My mother found me the next morning, sprawled out on the kitchen floor with half a bottle of pain pills scattered all around me. They found the empty bottle lying close-by and immediately began to suspect the worst, that I had taken an overdose of pills.

For me, everything was dark and indistinct. I could hear sounds but they were muffled and unclear. I could hear voices but I couldn't understand what was being said. For some reason I couldn't speak or move or even open my eyes. The world had become, for me, an endless blur of gray nothingness through which distant sounds could be heard, but not understood. I listened, trying to make some sense of it all, but the sounds were as gray and empty as the fog that surrounded me.

I listened.

And finally some of the sounds began to make sense to me.

The sounds were familiar in some way. I had heard them before. The sounds, I began to understand, were voices. The voices were talking about the pills. The voices were worried. They wondered how many pills I had taken. They thought that maybe that was the reason I was sick. I knew that I had to tell them that everything was okay, that I had only taken one pill, because I had a headache.

I had to tell them this so they would stop worrying.

This was important. They had to know. And because it was important and because they had to know, the fog seemed to dissipate for just a moment, and I was able to move the fingers of my right hand. With my eyes still closed, I made a fist, and extended my index finger alone. And I said, as distinctly as I could, so that they would understand.

I said, "I just took one."

The voices seemed to quiet for a time, but then came back, still concerned about the pills. So again, I said, "I just took one."

Then the world blurred into gray fog again and finally everything went completely black and silent. Occasionally the world would come back, now and again, as gray and indistinct as it was before, and when it did come back, I would listen to see if I could understand what was happening. The voices would fade in and out, sometimes different, sometimes the same, and every time the subject of the pills came up I always managed to make a fist with my right hand, extend my right index finger alone and say, "I just took one."

Eventually the voices stopped talking about the pills and I fell asleep.

I woke up about a month later. When I woke, they told me that I had had a brain hemorrhage and that I was very lucky to be alive. Only one in eight people usually survived it. They kept me in the hospital for another month, for rehabilitation and observation.

For the month that I had been in a coma, they kept me in a prone position, lying flat on my back, because they weren't sure what had caused the hemorrhage and they wanted to make sure that it had healed. This was back in 1968 and they didn't have all of the advanced medical technology and procedures that they do today. As I grew up, I completely forgot about falling out of the tree, and didn't really put the two events together until I was in high school.

I told my mother when I finally figured it out and she said, "Why didn't you tell me this before?" I hadn't realized how guilty she had felt about it all this time. For some reason she believed that my getting sick had been her fault. I said, "Sorry, I didn't really think about it until now. It just didn't seem all that important at the time. I fell out of a tree. Kids are falling all the time."

And life went on.

But it went on a little differently than it had been going before.

Because I hadn't remembered about falling out of that tree until much later, and because no one seemed to know why I would suddenly have a brain hemorrhage for no reason at all, I was told that I could not run or play or jump or do anything that might cause it to happen again.

And if you know anything at all about children, that's asking quite a lot from a kid who is only in the second grade. But I did it, and it wasn't so bad. I learned how to observe people and I was always looking around for ways that I could be useful. I would turn the jump rope for the girls during recess, or pick up litter on the playground, or talk to the grown-ups to see what life was really all about.

But the biggest change in my life was myself.

Before I went into the hospital I was a typical kid in the second grade. I could run fast. I could throw and catch a football pretty good. The girls liked me and I liked them. But afterwards, none of that stuff really seemed to matter. I found that I was more interested in knowing why things worked the way they did. I wanted to understand everything about the world. I wanted to know all that there was to know. And just telling me about it wasn't good enough. You had to be able to prove it to me in order for me to believe it.

Eventually this profound sense of doubt came to include my belief in God as well. No one could prove to me that God existed, so I didn't believe in Him. This was not to say that I was an Atheist (not yet, any way, though later I was). It just seemed to me that everyone was just as doubtful as I was; they didn't know if God really existed either, they just didn't want to admit it. I felt that if they really did know about God, like they said they did, then everyone else in the world would know it too and there would only be one religion. But there wasn't just one religion. There were all kinds. Even the Christians couldn't seem to decide on which Christian version of The Bible was really the right one.

So how was I supposed to know which one was the right one if the people who believed in it couldn't decide among themselves who was really right? So I began to think that no one really knew if any of it was true and that the whole thing was just make-believe and wishful thinking. I began to believe that the believers were just like me; they didn't really know anything either. They were just pretending that they knew because they were afraid of going to Hell.

At least that's how it seemed to me.

As I grew older and we moved again, I really began to wonder about those people who claimed to believe in God, because back in the 1970s some of those Christian people on the West Side of Jacksonville, Florida could be pretty mean. But as I think back on it now, I realize that it had only been a hundred years since the Civil War, and culturally speaking, a hundred years is not very much time at all, so quite naturally, they were all still pretty upset about it.

But as a kid, growing up in that place, I didn't think about it like that. The only thing I was thinking about was, if these people really believed in God and in Jesus the way they said they did, then how could they be so mean?

Didn't they see what Jesus was trying to tell them, I wondered, to love your enemy? What good was "believing" in God if you didn't believe in love? Wasn't God supposed to be all about love? It just didn't make any sense to me.

Didn't these people know that God was watching them? Apparently not, so I learned how to run fast and to watch my back.

School was really confusing because my memory wasn't that good. Whenever the teacher finished explaining something on the blackboard and she said, "Does anyone have any questions?" I was always the kid who raised his hand, and of course, the rest of the class would groan, "Not again!" Later on I found out that they didn't really understand it any better than I did. They just didn't care as much about it as I did.

But because my memory was so bad, I learned how to take meticulous notes and I learned how to outline chapters and summarize complicated ideas so that I could understand them. This served me well later in high school and later in life when I joined the Navy and went into their Nuclear Power Program, where I eventually wound up serving as a machinist mate in the engine room of a nuclear submarine for a good part of my six-year enlistment.

I think the most important thing I did while I was in the Navy was that I got baptized in 1982. God still hadn't revealed Himself to me and I was getting a little tired of waiting for Him to do something. I was firmly agnostic by then. I didn't know if God did or did not exist. And I was beginning to think that I would never know, so I decided to put God on the spot.

I decided that I would get baptized and that I would do my best to do everything that Jesus taught in the Bible to see what would happen. I also began a course of personal study, which led me to eventually read the Bible, cover to cover, twice while taking notes and studying other secular books about Bible history. This took about four or five years. And at the end of it, I was done. I had searched, but had not found. I had knocked, but no one had answered.

I wasn't worried about dying because I knew that I had an ace in the hole. I had been baptized and I had tried to live my life as Jesus had instructed his disciples to live theirs. This was very easy for me to do because I didn't seem to have any of the desires that the rest of the men in the world seemed to have.

I often wondered if maybe the brain hemorrhage I had had as a child might have had something to do with that. I didn't drink alcohol. I didn't smoke cigarettes. And I didn't go out to bars to try to pick up women that I barely knew for a date.

It was my belief, even while I was in the United States Navy, that if you weren't planning on marrying the girl, then you shouldn't even be kissing her. Most of the guys thought that this way of thinking was a little crazy, but every now and then one of them would come up to me and say, "Garrett, don't ever change," or, "Garrett, you're the most together guy I ever met." I remember this one guy who I worked with in the engine room saying to me, "What are you doing down here in Engine Room Lower Level? Shouldn't you be up on some mountain top somewhere dispensing wisdom?"

I said, "Well yes, I was up on that mountain top, but no one was going up there to see me, so I thought that maybe I should come down here for a while and see what the problem was." I was only joking, of course. You did a lot of joking when you were underneath the water for two months at a time inside a Nuclear Submarine.

Whenever anyone would ask me what my job was in The Navy, I would often say to them, " I'm basically a plumber, except for the fact that the water is radioactive." Or I would say, "I work inside the Large Intestine of a Nuclear Submarine," which was not too far from the truth. Because if you think about it, all those men on that submarine are eating food, and drinking milk and water, and even more coffee, so you can pretty well imagine, that they were also going to the restroom too.

Now if you don't know too much about submarines, you may wonder where all that stuff goes when they flush the toilet. Well, where it goes, is down into these big steel tanks called Sanitary Tanks which, over the course of a few weeks start to get pretty full, and so someone has to empty them. And as you've probably already guessed by now, it was I to whom this glorious job was given.

There were a number of these Sanitary Tanks on board the submarine, and I was tasked, from time to time, with the responsibility of emptying the one located in the compartment known as Machinery II, Lower Level. As I said, I wasn't kidding. I worked inside the Large Intestine of a Nuclear Submarine.

Well anyway, after six very long years in the United States Navy, I finally got out, and I returned home to Jacksonville, Florida to help my mom, because my father had divorced her for no good reason. And in those days, women who were married to men who served in the Navy couldn't get any part of their retirement after the men divorced them, even though their wives had raised their children and had taken care of their properties while they were at sea.

This seemed very unfair to me, and I felt that somebody should do something about it, and since I knew that I couldn't do anything to change the law fast enough to make a difference for my mom, I did the only thing that I could do to make things right. I made sure that she got all of the things that her husband had promised her while she had been married to him while he was in the Navy.

After I got out of the Navy, I thought about going into nursing, because I was pretty tired of working on machines, so I got a job as an orderly at Methodist Hospital at night, while I went to college in the daytime. But I quickly realized that nursing didn't appeal to me as much as I thought it would, and so I went to college to learn how to program computers.

When I graduated from college, I got a job as an electronic technician and did that for about twelve years. During that time I continued to try to live my life as Jesus had lived his life, not because I was afraid of dying and going to Hell, but because it seemed to me to be a good way to try to live a life.

Eventually I decided that if God was going to send me to Hell because I honestly did not know if He existed, then so be it, because if that was the way

God really was, then I was very sure that I didn't really want to have anything to do with Him.

Fairly often, while I was living with my mom, people would come to the door to tell me about God. I always enjoyed talking to them, because I was still searching and I really wanted to know how they thought, and how it was that they had come to know that God actually existed.

I remember one person who came to my door and she told me that I too had faith.

"Really?" I said. "How's that? Because I don't feel like I have faith."

"Yes you do," she said again.

"How?"

She said, "You have faith that the sun is going to come up every morning."

"No, I don't," I said. "I just look out the window and when I see the sun, I say to myself, 'Looks like the sun's came up again today. I guess I'd better go to work.'"

Someone else said to me, "You do have faith. You believe in George Washington and you never saw him before. And you believe in the North Pole and I bet you've never been there either, have you?"

Now that one got me for a minute.

I had to stop and think about that.

It was true. I did seem to believe in those things without ever having seen them. Why was that? It was a very good question. I was intrigued. So I thought about it for a few seconds and then I realized why it was that I did believe in those things.

I said to him, "That's not faith; that's extrapolation! I see the ground. I can stand on it. I can touch it. I know it exists. I've lived in Maine. I've lived in Newfoundland. I know that it gets colder the further North you go. So the idea of The North Pole existing is something that I can logically believe in.

"The same is true of George Washington," I said. "George Washington was a man. I am a man. My father was a man. Both my grandfathers were men. So it's not so hard for me to believe that there were other men too—men who used to live on this planet before I was born, and that one of these men who was born long before I was, was named George Washington. And to be honest with you, I really don't know if Gorge Washington really did exist, but the probability that he existed seems very high to me, and so I believe in the possibility of his existence.

"But I have never seen any gods wandering up and down the streets here, or buying shoes at the shopping malls," I said, "so how can I extrapolate the existence of your God? I have nothing to compare Him to, nothing that I have ever seen with my eyes or heard with my ears or felt with my other senses. So how can I believe? How do you believe?" I said and eagerly awaited his reply, because I really wanted to know how he could believe in something that he had never seen, but he didn't have an answer.

He said that it was getting late and that he had to go.

That was my life. I lived with my mom, making sure that she got all of the things that she was promised to by her husband, but who had left her instead. And I started writing this book. We had a lot of nice times together. And when she grew old and the time came for her to die, we went to all of the old places that we remembered when we were growing up together. I took her to the movies and bought her popcorn and candy. We went for walks in the parks and the shopping malls. It was a very happy life.

I remember the last thing she said to me before she died.

She said, "Use a coaster. It will leave a mark."

I had given her a drink of water and I was about to set the glass on the coffee table, and that's when she said it. She said, "Use a coaster. It will leave a mark." I liked that. There were no tearful good-byes. She didn't say, "I'm proud of you," or, "I love you," because she had already said all those things to me while she was alive, and now that she was leaving, the only thing left for her to say before she went, was to, "Use a coaster. It will leave a mark."

So of course, I did.

And life without her went on for many years.

I never got married, because all of that romantic stuff that men and women do for each other never really appealed to me. It was too complicated having to remember birthdays and holidays and people's names. I always felt that I would have made an excellent priest if I had believed in God.

I knew one day that I would probably die.

That's just the way things seemed to work; everybody seemed to eventually wind up dying. But it didn't worry me too much because I felt that I had a plan. I decided that when I did die and I found myself looking up at God, face to face, I planned on whipping out my Baptismal paper with my name on it and saying, "What are you gonna do now? I got baptized; I tried to live my life as Jesus lived his. It was the best I could do. What are you gonna do now?"

I envisioned this really big argument between God and me, along the same lines as the one He had with Abraham, the one where Abraham questions God about destroying everyone in Sodom and Gomorrah. Abraham asks of God, "Will you sweep away the innocent with the guilty? Suppose there were fifty innocent people in the city; would you wipe out the place, rather than spare it for the sake of the fifty innocent people in it?"

Abraham eventually talks God down to ten people, and afterward agrees not to destroy Sodom and Gomorrah until Abraham can go there to save Lot and his family, who are good and righteous people. Reading this account of Abraham and God as a teenager, gave me some hope. It made me see that it was possible to win an argument with God providing that you were on the right side of the issue, and I believed that I was, so I wasn't too afraid to die.

I felt my chances were pretty good of winning my argument with God (if He really did exist), or at least succeed in convincing Him to have a second look about this whole faith idea. Not everyone in the world can believe in things by faith alone. Look at doubting Thomas, and he was an Apostle. He didn't believe that Jesus had risen from the dead until he saw for himself, and I was pretty sure that he wasn't burning in Hell for all eternity because of it.

Occasionally I would go to church when someone invited me, but going to church, for me, was the loneliest feeling in the world. All of the people there seemed to know something that I did not. They seemed so happy, and I did not want to disturb their happiness by asking them a lot of uncomfortable questions, so I would go with them and be very polite and smile pleasantly. And I'd drop a little money into the collection plate as it passed by.

Going to church, for me, was very similar to going to a party. I never liked going to parties either. All the people there seemed to be enjoying themselves so much, doing things that didn't really interest me at all. And so, in the midst of their revelry, I would look around and see that I really didn't belong there, and I would quietly bow out, and be sure to softly shut the door as I left.

My mother said that when I was born, and they pulled me out of her, that I didn't make a sound. The doctor slapped me on the butt, as they used to do in those days, and still I said nothing. So he slapped me again, this time a little harder and I said, "Wah." Just that, a short little cry, and then I went back to sleep. And that's how I figured I'd probably leave this world too, quietly, and without too much crying.

Besides, what was there to cry about?

I was born. I paid my taxes. I helped those people that I could, and I never took more from the pot than I put into it. In fact, I had planned on never taking anything from the pot because I didn't really ever seem to need anything. I had been so lucky to have been born whole (and not too ugly) to loving parents who cared about me. They weren't perfect, of course, but then who is? They did the best that they could with what they had. Quietly I had come into this world and quietly I would leave it.

And that was fine with me.

THE FIRST TIME I ALMOST GOT AN ANSWER

I remember the day I thought my time had finally come, the day when I would quietly bow out of the game of life. I was in the bathroom, doing what people usually do when they go to the bathroom, when suddenly I was beset with terrible stomach cramps. The cramps were so intense that I had to lower myself onto the floor and curl up into a fetal position just to endure the pain. As I lay there, curled up in pain, I noticed something about myself. I noticed that I was completely paralyzed. I could not move one single muscle in my entire body.

It was strange. Despite my helplessness, I was not afraid.

I was just lying there, on the floor, doubled over in pain, waiting for something to happen. And I remember thinking, "So this is it. I'm finally going to find out the answers to all The Great Questions I had during my lifetime: Does God really exist? What happens after we die? Was I going to see my mom again? Soon, I told myself. Very soon, I was about to find out. I was very intrigued by it all, as I lay there, waiting for what was about to happen next. Waiting to know the answers to my questions. Waiting in the dark, because my eyes were squeezed shut from the pain. I was waiting.

Waiting.

And as I waited, I began to notice something.

I began to notice that I could move the thumb on my right hand, just a tiny little bit. So I focused on that. I moved my thumb as much as I could, back and forth, back and forth, back and forth, until I could begin to feel the fingers on my right hand coming back to life. And soon, I found that I could make a fist.

So I began to do that.

I made a fist and I opened my hand, made a fist and opened my hand, again and again, until I could begin to feel my right arm coming back to life. And then I opened my eyes and I saw that I was not lying on the floor after all. I found myself in a squatting position, balanced on the tips of my fingers and the tips of my toes, coiled up, like a spring. A darkness seemed to lift from my mind and float away. I reached up to steady myself against the cabinet that held the sink.

The pain was gone.

I stood up slowly, leaning against the cabinet.

I stretched and looked at myself in the mirror.

I didn't look too bad, I thought. In fact, I looked pretty normal, and so I said to myself in the mirror, "Well I guess I'm not going to be finding out the answers to those questions today, after all. Maybe next time. Whenever that might be." So I finished what I was doing in the bathroom, got dressed, and went to work.

THE SECOND TIME I ALMOST GOT AN ANSWER

It was some time later and I was in the bathroom again, getting ready to go to work when I noticed a sensitive patch of reddened skin between my eyebrows. I pressed it and scrubbed it with soap and put some acne medication on it. I continued to watch it and medicate it for a few more days, but it didn't seem to be going away. The next day when I woke up to view it I saw that my right eye was swollen shut.

"Oh-oh," I said. "This is definitely not acne." So I hopped in the car and drove down the street to see a doctor. The doctor told me that it was shingles.

I said, "Is there a cure?"

She said, "Yes."

I said, "Quick, give it to me!"

And she did.

The cure, it turns out, was a bag full of pills, three different kinds of pills, with three different frequencies, plus eye drops, because the shingles had gotten into my right eye. So I put all of these medications on top of the coffee table in the living room, next to an alarm clock that I would use to keep track of the time. I would sleep in the living room on the sofa, next to the coffee table, until I got better.

The thought of calling someone to help me, or letting anyone know (besides work) that I was sick, didn't even occur to me. I mean, what were they going to do about it? Hold my hand and tell me everything was going to be okay? Nawh, I wasn't going to do that. Most of the people I knew had enough problems of their own. I wasn't going to burden them with my mine. I was fine. Besides, what was the worst that could happen? I could die. And I was ready for that.

On the third day of the treatment, I woke up suddenly in the middle of the night. I looked around the living room, wondering what had awakened me. I saw nothing, so I got up and looked out the window, but I didn't see anything out there either. I went back to the sofa, fluffed up the pillow, and went back to sleep.

Suddenly I was awake again.

This was strange.

So I tried again to sleep, but this time as I began to fall asleep, I made an effort to be completely aware of what was happening to my body. My heartbeat slowed, my breathing slowed, my mind was lazily drifting off to sleep and suddenly I was awake again!

But this time I knew what was happening.

As soon as I had entered the first stage of sleep, I noticed that I had stopped breathing! So I tried it again, just to be sure. I let myself start to drift back to sleep again. And again, I stopped breathing! Okay, now I knew the problem, so of course, I decided to do another test. I slowly drew in a deep breath of air and held it. Next, as part of my test, I was going to release it slowly, but as soon as I tried to do that, all of the air came rushing out of my lungs. I had no control over how I exhaled my breath!

Ah, now this was very interesting, I thought.

But what do I do next?

When I was fully awake I seemed to have complete control over my breathing, so what was I going to do? Stay awake all night? No, that wasn't feasible. I thought about trying something else, a different kind of test maybe.

Maybe if I turned on the TV set, it would activate a part of my brain that would keep me breathing as I began to fall asleep again. So I grabbed the remote and turned on the TV, and behold, what appeared on the screen of my TV set? It was Jesus smearing clay on the eyes of a blind man to heal him (It was a commercial for this new movie that had come out in the theaters. It was called *The Book of John.*).

I lay there on the sofa for a moment, wondering what I should do next. Was God trying to send me a message? Was He trying to communicate with me in some new way? Was He trying to tell me to crawl off the sofa and place my hands on the screen of the TV set and say, "I believe?" What if I did do that and I did get healed? What would that prove? Would it prove that God existed?

But what if I did nothing instead? What if I just lay there on the sofa and did nothing at all to see if I would be healed without asking God for anything? Wouldn't that be a better test?

I thought so.

And if I got better, what would that prove?

I wasn't sure. But I had to know one way or the other.

So I stayed there, on the sofa, and let the TV run all night long. The next morning, when I woke up, I was okay. That is, I could breath normally again when I slept. I still had shingles on the right side of my face, and it was still pretty painful, but I was alive. Maybe I would have been cured of my shingles too if I had decided to crawl up to the TV set last night, I thought, but now I would never know.

I wondered what had happened; what had caused me to stop breathing? Maybe I had lost track of all the medication I was taking and had taken one two many pills and it suppressed my breathing reflex. I wasn't sure. As for the existence of God, I wasn't sure about that either.

But one day I finally did get an answer.

And, interestingly enough, it came in the form of:

AN OIL CHANGE

I was sitting in the waiting room of one of those fifteen-minute-quick-change-oil places, waiting for the guy who was working on my car to come into the waiting room to tell me that I needed to have my air filter changed, or my transmission fluid replaced. But instead, a young woman dressed in a nurse's uniform, white with red stripes like the kind that candy stripers who do volunteer work at hospitals wear. She came up very close to me smiling pleasantly. She said, "Would you like a breathing treatment?"

I was a little surprised by this question because, as I said earlier, I used to work as an orderly at Methodist Hospital on the North side of Jacksonville while I was going to college. And I knew that they didn't let just anybody do a breathing treatment. You had to be a certified respiratory therapist in order to give a breathing treatment. And if you were a certified respiratory therapist who was qualified to give breathing treatments, then what were you doing working at a fifteen-minute-quick-change-oil place?

I was just getting ready to ask her this question, when she popped a plastic vinyl tube into my mouth and switched on the breathing treatment machine.

So there I was, sitting in a fifteen-minute-quick-change-oil place, getting a breathing treatment!
 I was very perplexed about the whole thing.
 When she was done, I asked her what was going on.
 She said, "It's the newest thing. Everybody's giving them these days."
 "Really?" I said.
 "Oh yes," she said.
 And she was right.
 After I finished getting the oil in my car changed, I went to a local supermarket that was just across the street, and I was standing in line with my items when the cashier came up to me and said, "Would you like a breathing treatment?"
 I said, "I just got one while I was getting my oil changed."
 She said, "It never hurts to have another one. It's very good for your lungs. Everyone is getting them these days."
 "That's just what the girl at the oil-change place said," I said.
 "Well she was right," the cashier said, and she inserted a plastic mouthpiece attached to some vinyl tubing into my mouth and switched on a machine that was sitting next to her cash register. And there I was, standing in line, getting another breathing treatment, and I was thinking, "How strange. When did all this start happening? I didn't see anything about it in the newspapers or on TV."
 I went to work the next day, still thinking about that, and everyone at work kept asking me how I was doing. They said they had heard how I had gotten hurt while I was working some overtime at another branch of the supermarket chain I worked for, and they wondered if I was okay.
 I said, "I don't know where you heard that, but I'm just fine."
 Then I went to Aisle Six to start to work, stocking groceries, which was odd, because I didn't work in Aisle Six. I worked in the Produce Department, but for some reason no one seemed to care that I had gone to Aisle Six instead. I didn't think much about it either, for some reason.
 That went on for a few more days. I would go home and go to bed and sleep, and I would get up the next day, and go to work in Aisle Six, stocking groceries. And everyone I met would ask me if I was okay, and I would say, "Fine, as far as I know."
 After about a week of stocking groceries in Aisle Six, I began to have the strangest feeling. It was a feeling that I had often had throughout my life. It was the feeling that I was not really awake, that I was dreaming.
 Not to bore you with my dreams, but let me give you a quick example of what I mean: One sunny, blue sky, summer day, I was riding my skateboard to the store at the end of the street (It was called Tanner's Store, because that was the name of the man who owned it.) and I was being pursued by a large green scaly dragon. Now all of this made perfect sense to me at the time, except for the fact that the skateboard wasn't going fast enough.

So I hopped off the skateboard and picked it up and turned it over to have a look at the wheels. But instead of having wheels, the skateboard had a bent up coat hanger nailed to the spot where the wheels should have been. This seemed to make perfect sense to me. So I put the skateboard back down on the road, got back on, and continued my journey towards Tanner's Store, with the big green dragon still in pursuit.

When I got to the end of the street, I found that my car, a 1987 Ford Bronco II, was parked in front of the store, so I got inside. My younger sister, Vanessa, was sitting in the passenger side seat. I looked at her and saw that she was twelve years old. And that caused me to stop and think, because I knew that my sister was not twelve years old. She hadn't been twelve years old for quite some time. In fact, she was twenty-three years old. And then I knew that I was dreaming!

Whenever I had a dream like this, when I could realize that I was dreaming while I was still asleep, I could do pretty much as I pleased in the dream. Most times when I realized that I was dreaming, I would fly away to some distant place across the ocean or above mountain tops or even sometimes to distant planets, but not too often. For some reason it was very hard to break away from the Earth's influence. I went to the moon a few times, never to the sun.

But the point is, there I was, stocking groceries in Aisle Six, and I had begun to suspect that I might be dreaming, and so I did what I usually did when I thought I might be dreaming. I started looking for clues.

I called my younger sister, Vanessa, on the phone and I told her that I thought I might be dreaming. We talked for a while and I said goodbye and soon it was time to go back to work in Aisle Six. But now I was suspicious.

Now I suspected that none of it was real.

Sometimes, when I suspected that I might be dreaming, but couldn't find any clues to give me definitive proof, I would do a kind of "reality test." The test that I would usually use was "to see if I could fly." If I could rise up into the air and fly away, then I knew that I was dreaming.

But even this test was a little tricky sometimes.

One time, when I was asleep and I suspected that I was dreaming, and I tried to test it by flying, all I could manage to do was to jump over the roof of our house. But in the dream, jumping over the roof of the house seemed perfectly normal, so it didn't prove anything to me.

So I kept trying to jump higher and higher and higher until eventually, I jumped so high above the house, way up into the clouds, that my mind was forced to accept the fact that I was dreaming. But for some reason, while I was standing there in Aisle Six, suspecting that I might be dreaming, the thought of testing it by flying hadn't occurred to me, until I got home later that night and found myself in bed.

The room seemed oddly different as I sat up in my bed looking at it. In fact, it looked nothing at all like my bedroom. There were no windows. There was no furniture. There was no ceiling. It was just myself, sitting in the middle of a plain white mattress, surrounded by an empty expanse of white nothingness that expanded outward, away from me, on all sides.

For some reason, all of this seemed very normal to me, though I suspected that it was not. Now, I said to myself, was the time to do my test to see if I was dreaming. I would try to rise off the mattress and fly off to some distant land across the ocean or above the mountains. But for some reason, no matter how hard I tried, I could not fly, which left me believing that everything that I was experiencing must be real.

Even so, I wasn't completely convinced, so I kept trying.

I sat straight up in bed and concentrated very hard.

When suddenly, the entire mattress rose up into the air!

And now I knew I was dreaming.

Okay, one mystery solved.

But why couldn't I wake up?

Where was I?

What was happening out there in the real world?

I had to wake up. I had to find out.

I had to find some way of getting out of the dream. I had to wake up and get out of bed. But, for some reason, no matter how hard I tried; I remained in the dream. What was wrong? What was happening out there in reality?

REALITY

What was happening out there in reality was this: I had suffered another subarachnoid brain hemorrhage, just as I had when I was in my second year of elementary school after I fell out of that gumball tree. But this time I had been working overtime at the 103rd street branch of the supermarket chain that I worked for. My brother, Keith, told me later that whoever I had been working with at the time said that I had been working normally, putting things away, when suddenly I just fell to the floor and passed out.

I don't remember any of this.

I don't even remember going into work that night. The first thing that I remember was that I was sitting in the waiting room of that fifteen-minute-quick-change-oil place. My brother Keith told me later, that after I had collapsed, I had stopped breathing. My co-workers called an ambulance, and luckily, there had been an ambulance close-by, and they were able to get me hooked up to a respirator before any serious brain damage occurred.

They took me to Shands Hospital on the north side of Jacksonville City, where they shaved my head, drilled holes into my skull to drain the blood that was filling up my brain. They intubated me. They catheterized me. They scanned me. They kept me doped up on morphine to keep my blood pressure down. I had vinyl tubing coming out my skull, vinyl tubing going into my lungs, vinyl tubing going into the veins in my arms, vinyl tubing going into the veins in my groin, and vinyl tubing going up and into places I don't even want to think about.

But I knew nothing of this. I was in a coma and had absolutely no idea what was happening out in the real world. I was alive. That was all I knew. I was alive and trapped inside of a dream that had no exit. But I had a plan. I had a plan that I believed would help me to figure out a way to get out of the dream and to find reality again.

The dream was shifting and changing now, as my subconscious mind began to realize that I was in the hospital. My bedroom morphed into a maze of sterile white hallways that zigzagged around in all kinds of crazy directions. I remained seated squarely in the middle of my flying mattress, methodically flying up and down the surreal looking hallways looking for a way out of the dream. My subconscious mind had apparently picked up on the fact that my wrists were strapped to the railings on the bed to keep me from pulling out the tubes that were inserted into my body. That was the reason the bed rose up with me when I had attempted to fly away from it.

Again, I knew nothing of this, until much later.

But this was my plan. Now that I knew that I was dreaming, I would fly the bed all through the maze of hallways and rooms, until I found a place in the dream where the bed would not fly. That, I decided would be the place that would lead me to reality, because beds don't fly in the real world.

And so, I was off, flying my bed, through the maze of hallways and rooms, searching for reality. I flew that bed all around that hospital for about a month while I was hooked up to a respirator, looking for reality.

As time progressed, I am told that my condition steadily improved. The doctor that was tending me began to consider removing me from the ventilator, but he was hesitant. He wasn't sure what might happen. It was during this time that my conscious mind was slowly beginning to realize where it was, and I began to think, "I can't afford this! Get me out of here!" My sister said that I somehow managed to get loose from my restraints and I pulled out the respiratory tubing myself.

During this stage of my journey, I was in and out of the dream. Sometimes I would be in a gray place, surrounded by a fog of unfocused light through which I could hear far away voices murmuring in hushed indistinct tones. Sometimes one voice would get close enough so that I could understand it, and I would talk to it. This voice I recognized as my sister, Vilita. I also remember talking frequently to another person all dressed in white, about God, and about how I had always wanted to believe in God, but for some reason was never able to.

As I became more aware of my surroundings, I could begin to hear all the beautiful voices of all the beautiful nurses who were taking care of me, and because I couldn't see their faces, my mind made up images to match their beautiful voices. In my mind, they were all perfect radiant angels in white robes. I don't remember if they had wings, but I do seem to remember something about wings.

During this part of my recovery, my sister told me that I asked every nurse on the floor to marry me. She said I asked her to marry me too and also my niece, Niki. I think they all turned me down. I don't remember any of this either, thank heavens.

One of the strangest things I remember seeing as I was flying my bed all around that hospital looking for reality, was this one place. It was a long dark rectangular hallway lined with hospital beds on both sides. The hallway and the beds seemed to go on forever. Some places in this hallway were dimly lit and other places were completely dark.

As I watched the beds more closely, I could begin to see faint images of ghostly people slowly materializing upon the mattresses beneath white linen blankets. The longer I watched these people, the more solid they became, until they were no longer transparent ghosts, but fully formed people.

Once they were solid and completely formed, these people would sit up, get out of bed, and join an endless stream of other people who were wandering up and down the hallway between the two rows of beds, looking, it seemed, for a place to sleep.

Once these people found a bed to their liking, they would go to it and sit on the edge of the mattress to test its comfort. If it pleased them, they would lift their feet off the floor, swing their legs up and onto the bed, cover themselves up with the white linen blankets, and go to sleep. As they slept, they would slowly start to flicker and to fade away, until the bed was empty again.

I stood there watching this strange parade for a very long time. And I remember thinking to myself, "So this is life; you're born, you leave, you wander around a bit, and then you come back and fade off to the place where you came from, wherever that was..."

After receiving this revelation, I was suddenly back in the gray place, the place I remembered as a child when I suffered my first brain aneurysm.

I could feel a mattress against my back.
I could feel a pillow beneath my head.
I opened my eyes
I sat up and I saw my sister, Vilita, watching me.
I said, "Finally, somebody I know!"
She smiled at me.

CHAPTER 2

When I woke from my first coma in second grade, I woke with a profound sense of doubt. When I woke from my second coma at age forty-eight, I woke with a profound sense that God really did exist, even though I never actually saw Him. I also had a profound sense that I had nothing to do with the fact that I had survived. It was all the people in the real world who knew me and who prayed for me that saved me. God had heard their prayers and that was the reason I had lived. This belief was not something that I hoped was true. It was something that I *knew* to be true.

So any time anyone would say, "We knew you'd make it, you're a fighter." I would correct him instantly, and say, "It wasn't me that saved me. It was you. You and all the people like you, who prayed for me. God heard your prayers and He answered them."

After surviving my first aneurysm, when I was in second grade, I used to look deep within myself and I knew that I didn't really know if God existed. And because I couldn't read other people's minds, I thought that this was how everyone else felt too. They didn't really know, just as I didn't really know. That's what I thought that faith was all about. I thought faith was about saying that you believed in God even when you knew that you didn't really know. But now I see how this was a misconception. Now when I look deep within myself, I know that God does exist. This is what faith is really about. It's about knowing that you know, without knowing *why* you know. I know that God exists. I'm not just hoping or wishing.

I know.

Wow.

THE SIXTH SENSE

This new knowledge of God's existence has given me a different perspective on life. People are always talking about ESP or a Sixth Sense, and now I see that there is a Sixth Sense. Most people have it, but some people do not. I believe that this Sixth Sense is the ability to feel God's presence in The Universe. Some people are born deaf, or blind, or crippled in some other way, and we don't judge them. But when someone is born without the ability to feel God's presence in The Universe, we do judge him.

We tell him that it's a choice to believe in God. That it is his choice to believe or *not* to believe. And if he doesn't choose to believe, then he's going to go to Hell for all eternity. That's like telling someone who is born blind that it's his choice not to know what the color blue looks like. And if he doesn't know what the color blue looks like, then he is going to Hell. It is no more a choice for someone to believe in God than it is a choice for someone who is born deaf to decide that he wants to hear. We don't say to someone who is born deaf, "Why have you chosen not to hear?"

But we do say it about someone who does not believe in God.

"Why have you chosen not to believe?"

Why would God do this? Why would God create a person with eyes that can't see, or ears that can't hear, or minds that can't feel His presence in the Universe? Jesus answered that question in this way. He said, "It is so that the works of God might be made visible through him."

A true disciple of Jesus Christ would never tell an Atheist or an Agnostic that he is going to Hell simply because he cannot believe in God. That's like telling a deaf person that he is going to Hell because he doesn't understand music, or a crippled person that he's going to Hell because he doesn't know how to dance, or a blind person that he's going to Hell because he doesn't know what the color blue looks like.

It's no different.

I know.

I know, because I have lived it.

After my first aneurysm I did not know if God existed.

After my second aneurysm I did know that God existed.

Was it a choice on my part?

No.

And that's funny.

Funny strange, that is, but also a little laughably funny too, because for the first month after I got out of the hospital I could not help but laugh (quietly and to myself so that people wouldn't think that I was too crazy) almost on a continual basis. I knew that God existed! And yet, I couldn't tell you why I knew that He existed. I just knew!

I still laugh about it today (quietly and to myself most of the time).

I lost my house. I lost my property.

I lost my car. I lost my independence.
I lost a whole lot of money. But I'm happy.
It's a nice feeling...knowing.

Well worth the price. As I tell those who ask, "I'd rather be a poor Catholic than a rich Agnostic any day. When I was Agnostic, those who believed always told me that believing was a choice. You either chose to "believe" or you chose not to "believe." It was free will. That's what they said. But they were wrong. I hadn't suddenly *decided* to start believing in God. It hadn't been a choice on my part. I just knew, just as I knew what color the sky was by looking at it.

For no reason at all, I suddenly began to *know* that God existed. And now that I did know, I still had one promise left to keep. As an Agnostic, I had always admired Jesus, as I had admired Gandhi and Martin Luther King. And I had always said to myself that if one day I ever did know that God existed, then I would become a Christian, a follower of Jesus. Well, now that time had come.

I did know God existed, so now the time had come for me to make that choice. It was time for me to choose to become Christian. But which Christian faith should I choose? There were so many. Which one was the right one? My sister was Catholic, so did that mean that I was going to become Catholic too?

No. Not necessarily.

Before I went into the hospital, I was a vegetarian. But my sister and her family ate meat. Did that mean that I was going to start eating meat too, just because I was living with them now? No. And I'm not a militant vegetarian. I don't judge people just because they choose to eat animals. Though I do wonder about them sometimes. If someone says, "I love chicken," I have to stop him, and say, "No, you love 'eating' chickens. I love chickens. That's why I don't eat them." Of course this does annoy them, but Oh well, I just can't stand by and say nothing when someone makes a crazy statement like that.

It's like one of those western movies that you see in the theaters. At the very end of the show, there's usually a disclaimer that says, "No animals were harmed during the making of this film." And I have to say, "Hey, wait a minute. I'm pretty sure that those actors ate lunch while they were making that film, and I'll bet some of them were eating hamburgers or fried chicken or ham sandwiches, so I have to say that, 'Yes, animals were definitely harmed in the making of that film!'"

Of course my sister says that that's why God made cows and pigs and chickens, to be eaten. I'm not so sure I believe her, so I'm still a vegetarian. There were plenty of Saints who were vegetarians too. I did eat meat for about a year after I first got out of the hospital because I was pretty confused and I didn't know what to think. But after about a year of eating animals, and my brain got better, and I slowly began to become myself again, I found that I just couldn't do it anymore, and so I went back to being a vegetarian.

Part of my confusion was due, in part, to having lost a great deal of my short-term memory. I'm not exactly sure how the brain works, but the way my brain seemed to be working was like this: A normal person looks into a room and sees and hears things happening, or he walks from Point "A" to Point "B," and he has about one minute of short-term memory in his brain to record this event.

Everything he sees and hears for this one minute is held in his short-term memory, and is eventually transferred into his long-term memory, so that he can use it at a later time, important information, like how to get to the bathroom so he can use the toilet.

The way my brain seemed to be working, however, was like this: Instead of having one minute of recording time in my brain for short-term memory, I had only a few seconds. So all of the information that was being stored in my tong-term memory from my short-term memory was so fragmented and disjointed that it made no sense to me at all.

For example, when I visited with my brother, Keith, his house was a complete mystery to me. It was a vast and complex maze of hallways, stairways, porches, and rooms, where none of the pieces fit together in any kind of order. To me it was a twenty-room mansion with hallways and stairways zigzagging in all kinds of crazy different directions.

There was a doorway at the bottom of the stairway that led to the second story, and if you went through this doorway, it led to a screened-in porch with a sitting area that looked out into the backyard.

A few months later, when I went to visit my brother again, I found that there was no doorway at the bottom of the stairway. The doorway that I had remembered being there, was actually a doorway in the kitchen, and it did lead out to the back porch, but when my mind remembered it, it remembered it out of place.

Why was that?

My theory is this: A person with normal short-term memory would remember the entire journey from the top of the stairs to the back porch door in the kitchen. And that entire journey would eventually be put into his long-term memory. But my short-term memory only had enough space to remember the part of the trip from the top of the stairs to the bottom of the stairs; and then from the bottom of the stairs to the entry into the kitchen; and finally, through the kitchen to the door that led to the back porch.

And then all of these fragmented pieces of short-term memory were reassembled and placed into my long-term memory in random order, which was why I remembered that door as being at the bottom of the stairs instead of being in the kitchen. As you might imagine, I really didn't like going anywhere unless I had a map.

The whole point of this story is to allow you to understand just how confusing everything was to me. I had other problems too. Besides having to learn how to walk again, everyone looked the same to me. My sense of time was all mixed up too. I would do something in the morning and think that I did it yesterday.

One of the biggest changes in my life was that I no longer remembered my dreams. I used to dream all night long and remember them. I would go on the most amazing adventures, flying here and there like some kind of superhero, but after the aneurysm, I no longer remembered my dreams. I thought I would miss those dreams, but I don't. Life is exciting enough without the dreams.

But where was I?

Oh, yes. Which Christian faith to choose?

As an Agnostic, I always marveled at all the different Christian religions. Why were there so many? The Bible was supposed to be God's revealed Word to man. It seemed to me that if God was going to give instructions to mankind and make sure that he got it right, then He would arrange the laws of physics and organic biology to make sure that no matter who translated the Bible, it would always translate exactly the same. That way there would be no mistake about what God was trying to tell man.

But that's not the way it worked. There were so many variations, so many different translations. In fact the Catholic Bible had 73 books and the Protestant Bible had 66 books. So somebody must have ignored that warning at the end of the Bible and either added something or taken something away.

As an Agnostic, it seemed very clear to me that all the Christians of the world were really Catholics, whether they chose to admit it or not. You had the traditional Roman Catholic Catholics and the Greek Orthodox Catholics, and then you had the Protestant Catholics, which included everyone else: The Methodist Catholics, the Baptist Catholics, the Mormon Catholics, the Lutheran Catholics, the Anglican Church Catholics, the Episcopalian Catholics, the Quaker and the Shaker Catholics, The Seven Day Adventist Catholics, and all the rest.

So the choice seemed pretty clear to me, since Christianity started with the Roman Catholic Church, then I would try to become a Roman Catholic Catholic, because it represented, in my mind, Christianity in its most basic form.

So that's the choice I made.

I am a Roman Catholic Catholic.

And I like it a lot, despite its flaws, because I know that the only reason that it is flawed is that it is made up entirely of men. And men are flawed. The Catholic Church is like a building. You can have the idea for a building or the plans for a building lay out on paper, but a plan for a building is not a building. In order to make a building you have to build it out of something real.

If you build it out of wood, it will rot. If you build it out of bricks, it will crack. If you build it out of ice, it will melt. If you build it out of steel, it will rust. Every material with which you choose to build is flawed. Every material has its own weakness.

The same is true of The Catholic Church. God was not satisfied with merely the idea of a church. He wanted to take that idea and turn it into something real. So He honored men, who are most certainly flawed, by choosing us to be the stuff with which to build His Church.

And I am flawed too.

And perhaps, a little annoying at times, if you can imagine that. I still ask a lot of questions, and I'm still not certain if you're telling me the truth unless you can prove it to me. I guess that comes from being an Agnostic for most of my adult life. So be forewarned, if you're a Catholic, and even if you're not, and I see you acting badly, I'm definitely going to be stopping you and asking you why.

Or if you are a follower of one of the Christian faiths, and I hear you making disparaging remarks about the teachings of another Christian faith because they don't quite believe exactly what you believe, I'm definitely going to be stopping you and saying to you, "What did Jesus say?"

Jesus said this. He said, "This is how you will know that you are my disciple, that you love one another." It's as simple as that. Human life is a very complicated process. God knows this. He created it. And to make sure that all men can have an opportunity to have a relationship with Him, He has given us many ways of reaching Him.

So no matter what religion you are, and even if you have no religion at all, even if you are an Atheist, when you love your neighbor as you would love yourself, you become a disciple of Jesus, whether you know it or not.

Because all love comes from God.

This is what Jesus said.

This is what unifies us.

This is what makes us holy.

www.ingramcontent.com/pod-product-compliance
Lightning Source LLC
Chambersburg PA
CBHW060503030426
42337CB00015B/1706